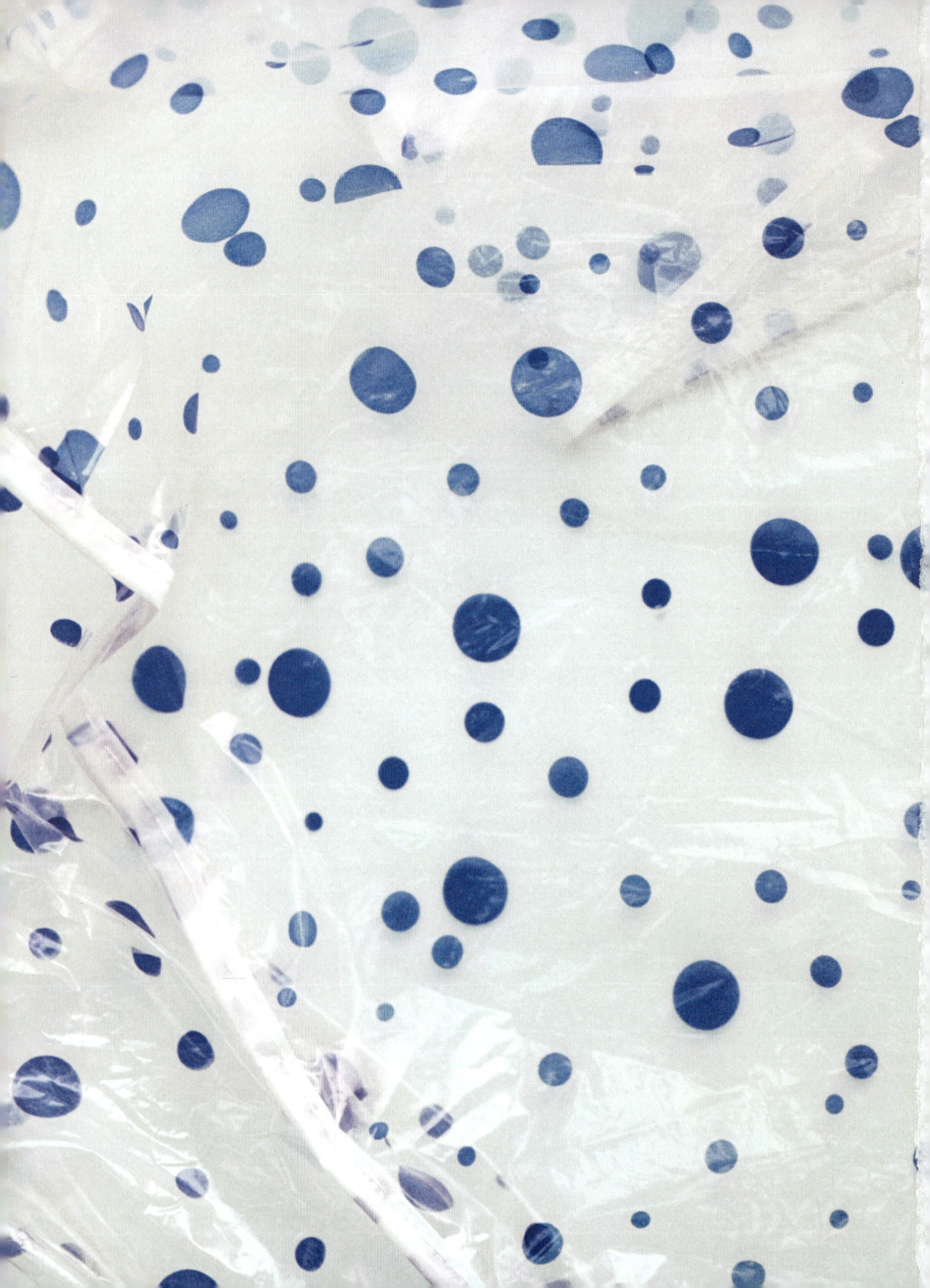

THE GRANNY ALPHABET

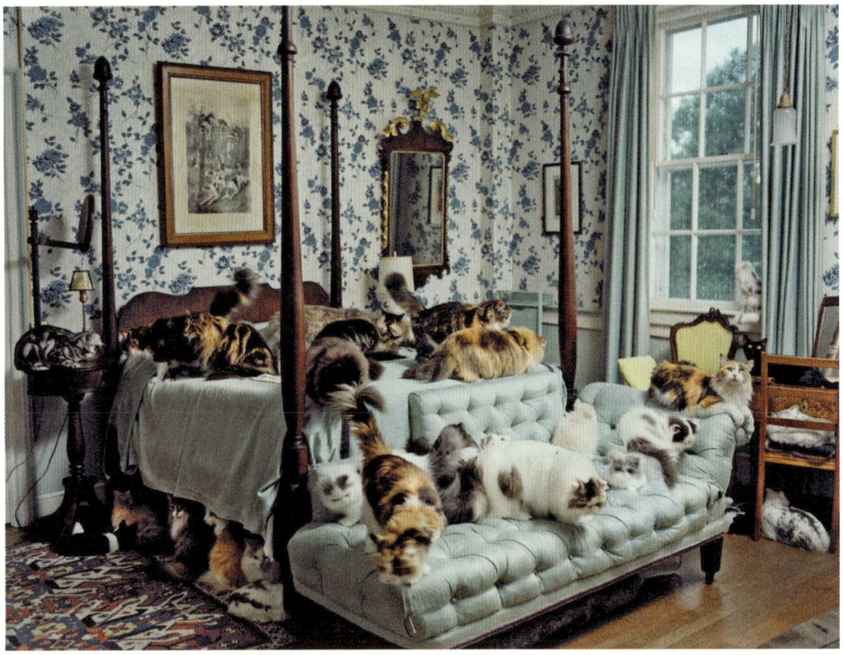

Thames & Hudson

THE GRANNY ALPHABET

PHOTOGRAPHS BY

TIM WALKER

VERSE BY

KIT HESKETH-HARVEY

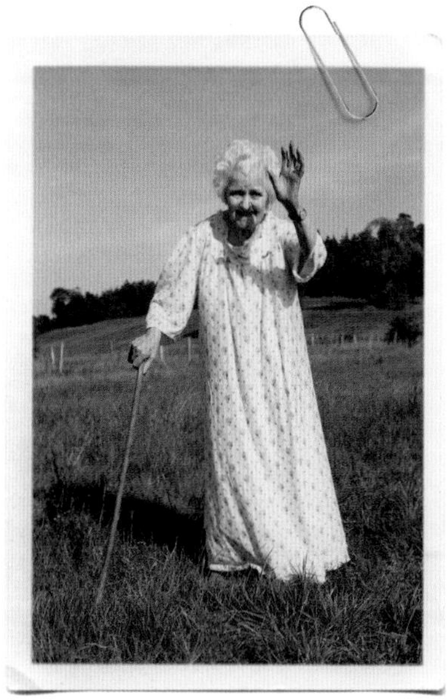

To Gamma, Louisa Wicks, 1995

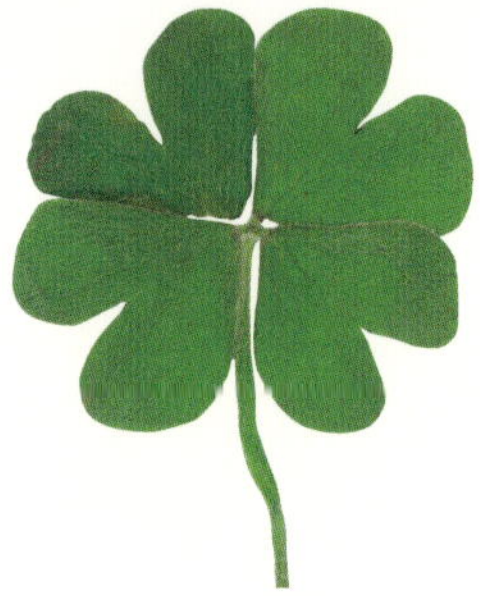

I've not been very good at growing up, but as I get older this seems to have been one of the better decisions life has made for me. To retain a child's eye when peering through the camera's viewfinder is to see the world as half magic, half horror. Old age brings back this childlike clarity of vision, and so children and the elderly have an agreement, a bond, united both by a sense of being out of time and by the brilliantly reckless lack of responsibility that bookends adulthood and allows them to see things as they really are. This is why I've always loved the very old and the very young, whether in age or spirit, and why I've taken the photographs for this book – part photographic love letter to the elderly and part documentation of the dying breed of little old ladies who live down the lane.

I am fortunate enough to have known both my grandmothers. My father's mother was called Grandma by my brother and me, Kathleen by others. She wore a brown fur coat over a jersey cream dress and when Grandpa took us out in his Triumph Dolomite to explore, she would put on her leather gloves to grip the handles of her shiny crocodile handbag. Their house was full of clocks that went tick-tock and chimed quarterly throughout the day as Grandma smoked her Silk Cuts and read us stories

about Captain Hook and Tiger Lily. In front of my grandparents' house stood a very large lime tree and I would spend hours beneath it searching for four-leaf clovers. Once I found one. I remember Grandma waving from the front door and saying, 'Good luck with your four-leaf clover…' But I'd already found luck.
I learnt the importance of luck from my other grandmother, my mother's mother, who my brother and I called Gamma, and others called Louie. One day Gamma and Poppa took us for a walk somewhere along the south coast of England. At one point, as they worked out from their map how to reach a flour-grinding windmill on a nearby hill, my brother and I were left to play on the edge of a crazy cliff. I can't quite remember how it happened but we ended up clambering and swinging on a rusting fence that hung out over the edge of the cliff – without Holden Caulfield to save us. Cradled in the rusting hammock of wire, I dropped torn pieces of tissue from my pocket and counted how many seconds they took to spiral down into the waves and rocks below. Gamma spotted us and waved her white hankie to get our attention. After inevitably scolding my brother and me for being so stupid, she laughed and said, as she always did, 'Better to be born lucky, than to be born rich…'

–T. W.

A is for Alphabet
(ABC),
And aged ancestors
(Awfully like me).
Twenty-six letters,
That's twenty-six Grannies.
Twenty-six photographs
(This one is Annie's).

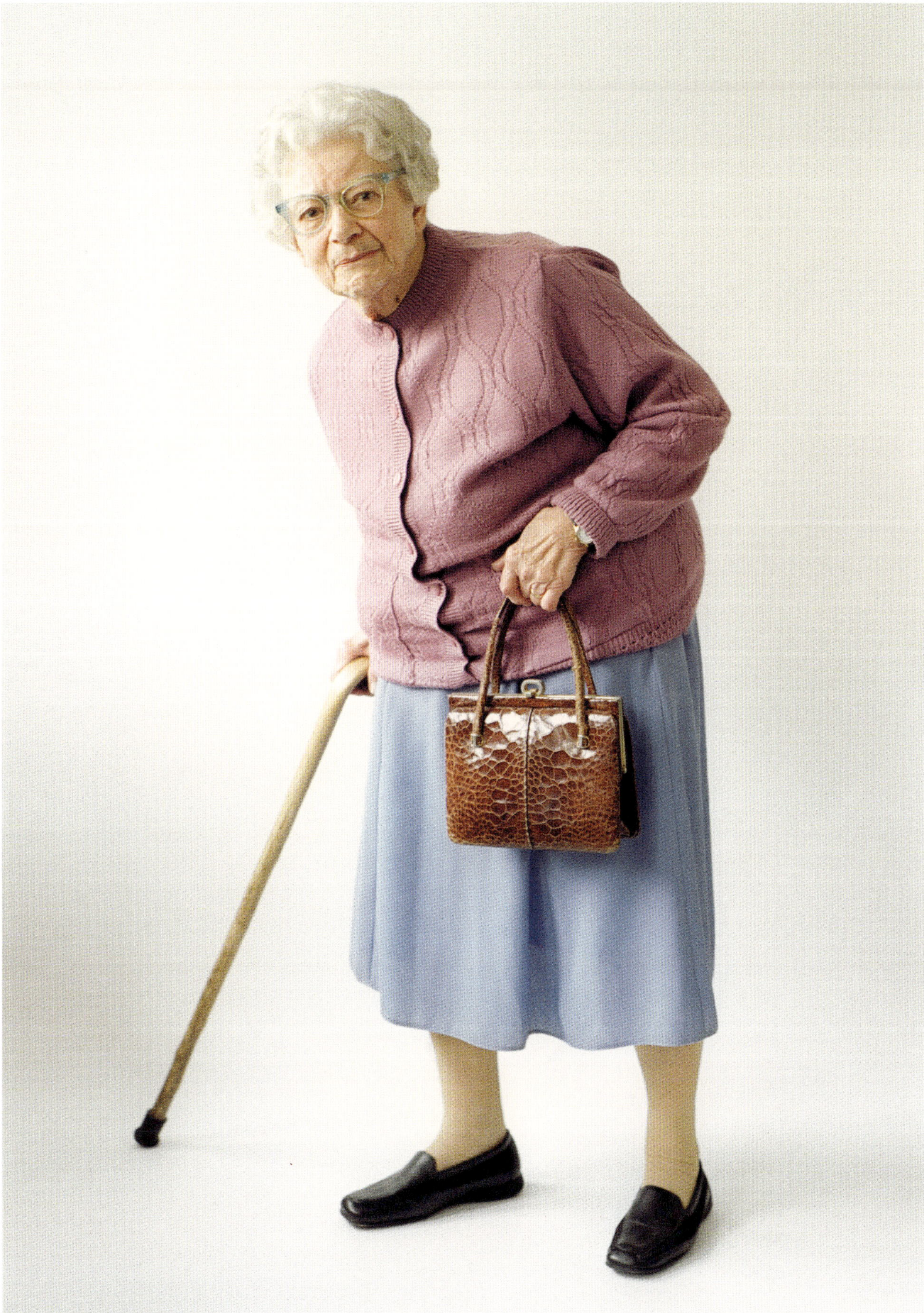

B

Brenda's bag is bulging,
A bunch of boring bills,
Bus passes and buttons and bright blue burping pills,
A bit of blossom, broken
From a branch at Becky Falls,
And, buried at the bottom,
By Jingo! Bingo balls!

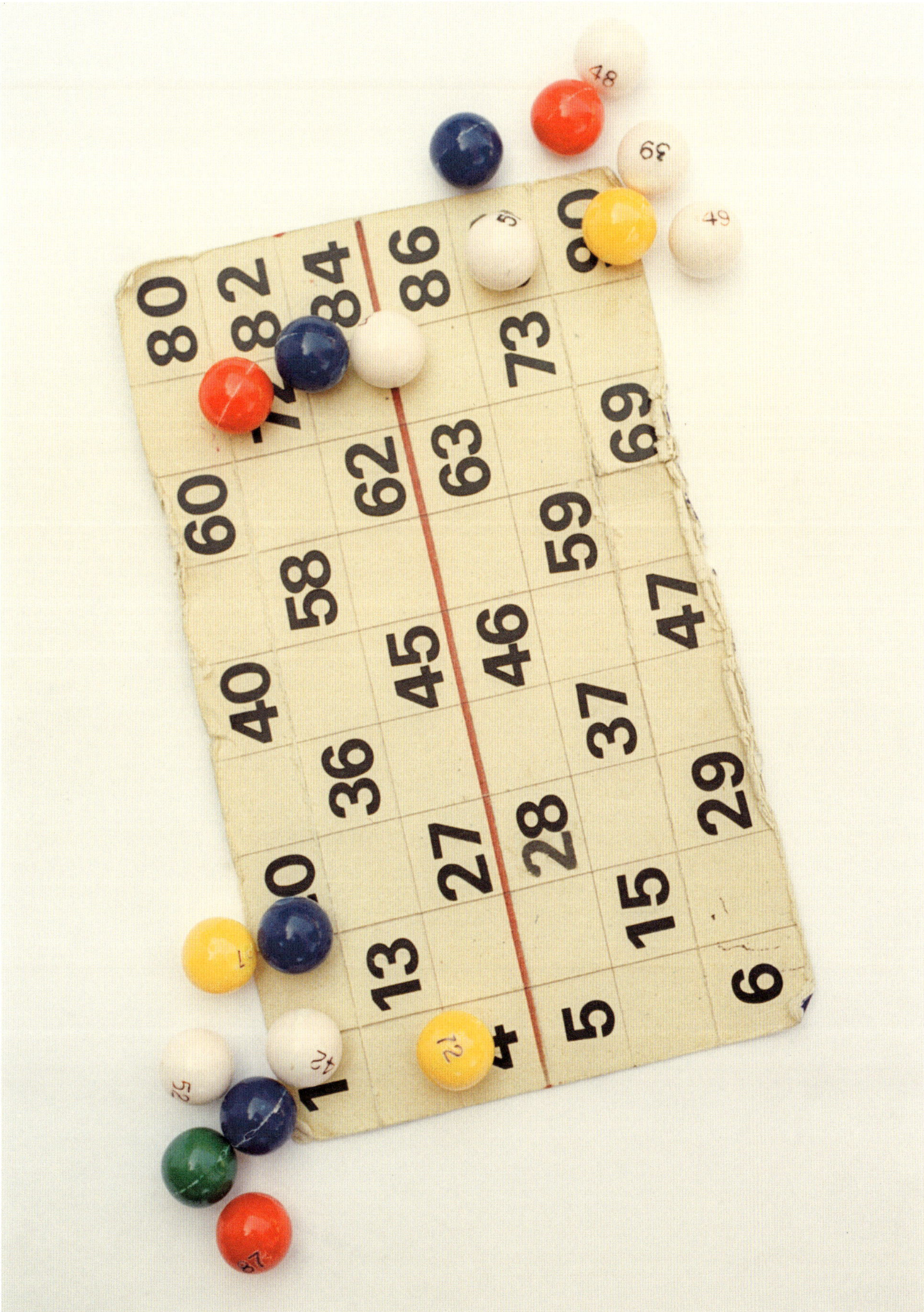

Carol's name's not cool at all,
Carol thinks it's dire.
At Christmas she puts on her cape,
And gets sung by the choir.

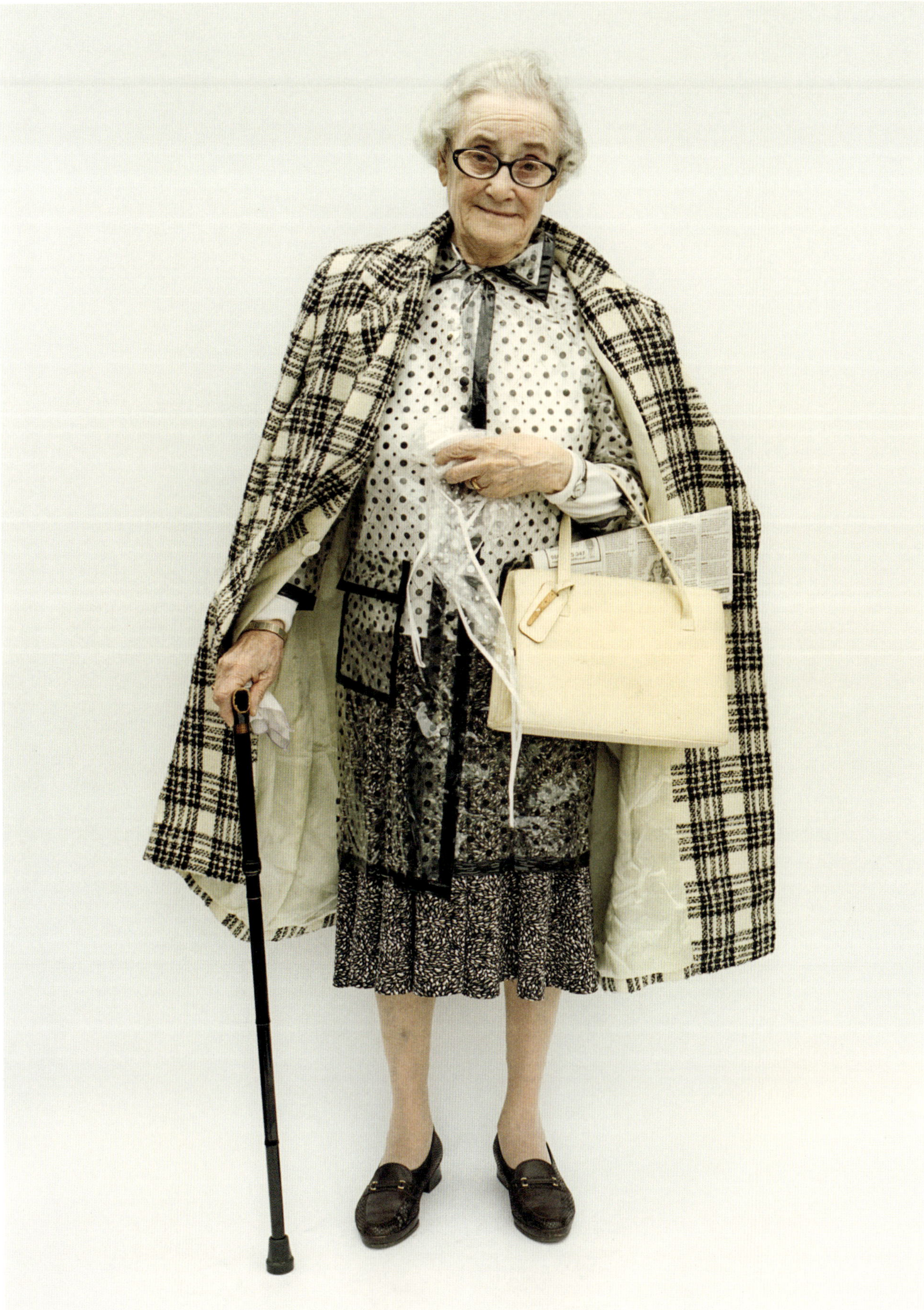

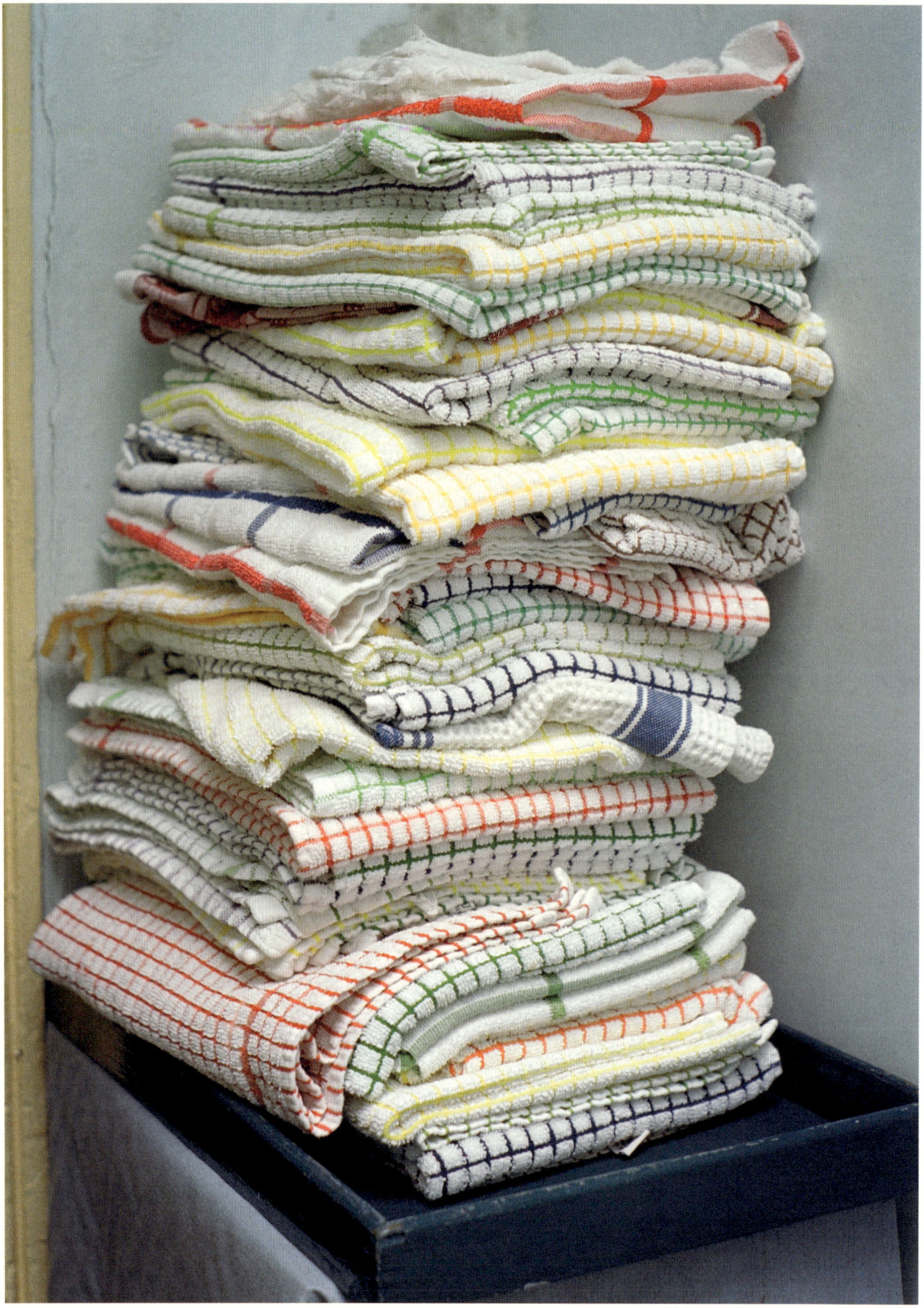

D

Dora has dozens of dishcloths
(Last count 110),
So if at first Dora doesn't succeed,
Dora will dry, dry again.

E

Everyone's looking for Enid,
No one's seen Enid for years.
She eloped with her lover to Egypt
(Ex-Army, Royal Engineers).
He was tusked by an elephant, R.I.P.
But everyone's asking,
'Where can Enid be?'

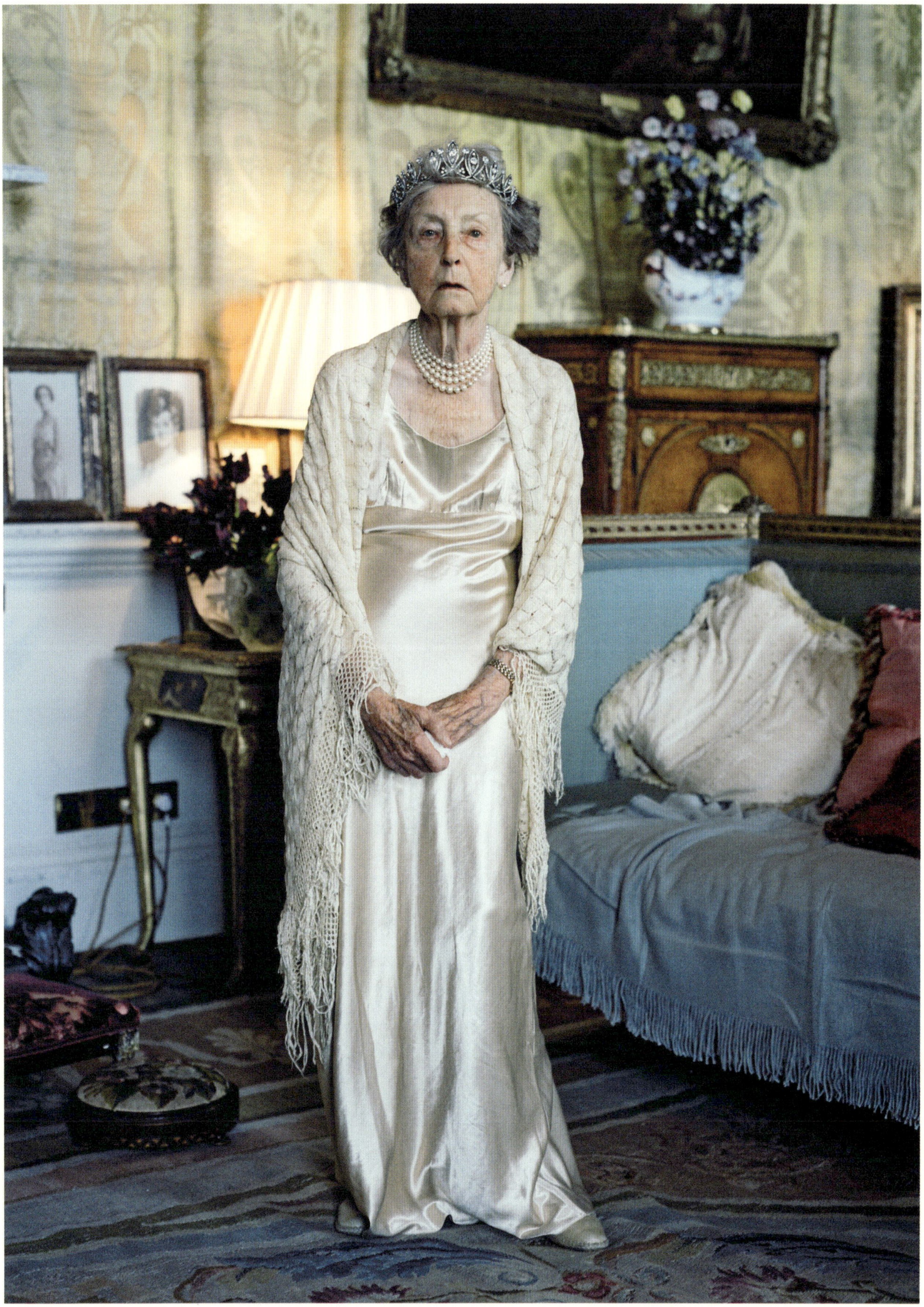

F

Fenella's false teeth,
O, fearful fright!
(I hope you brushed
And flossed tonight!)

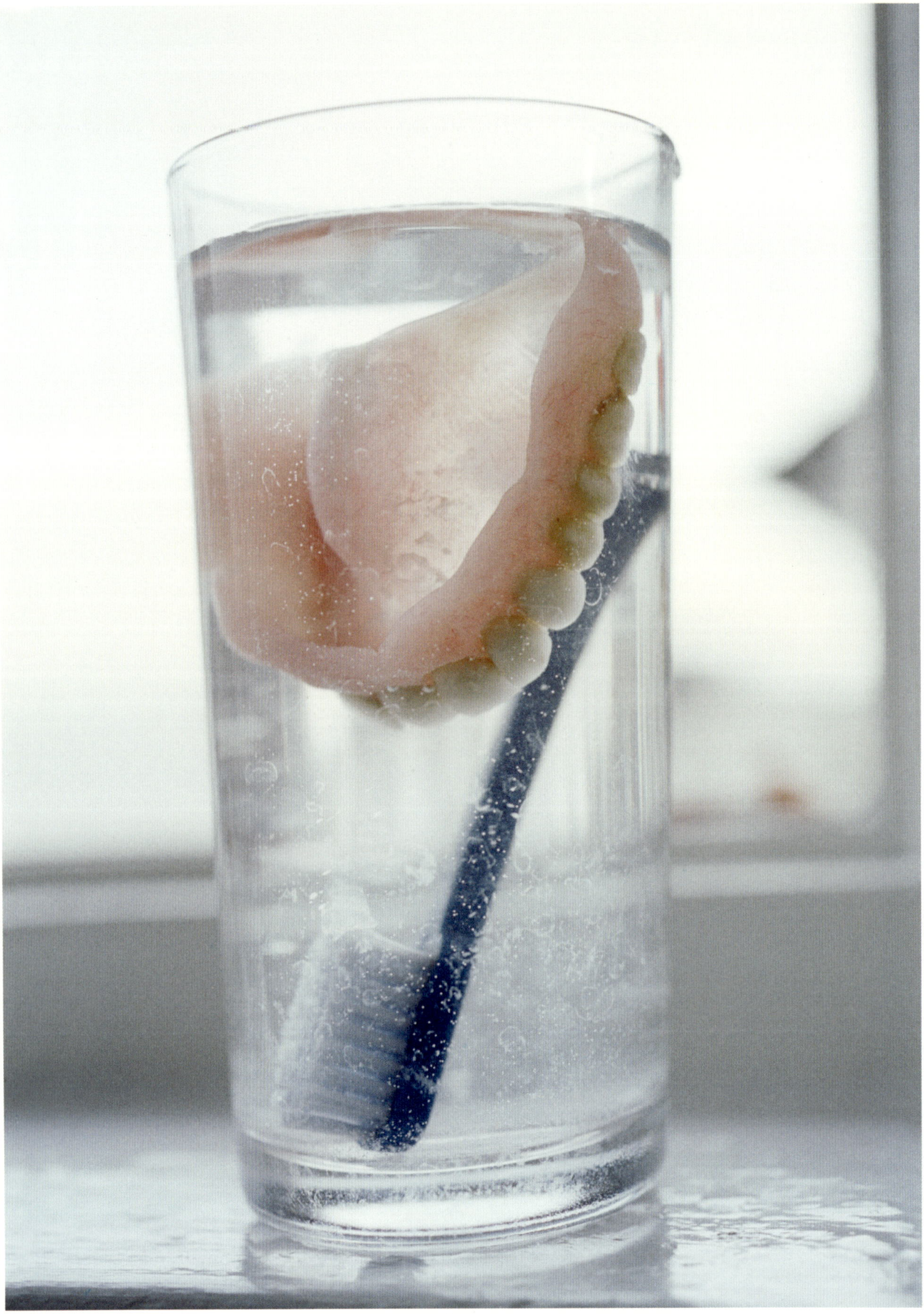

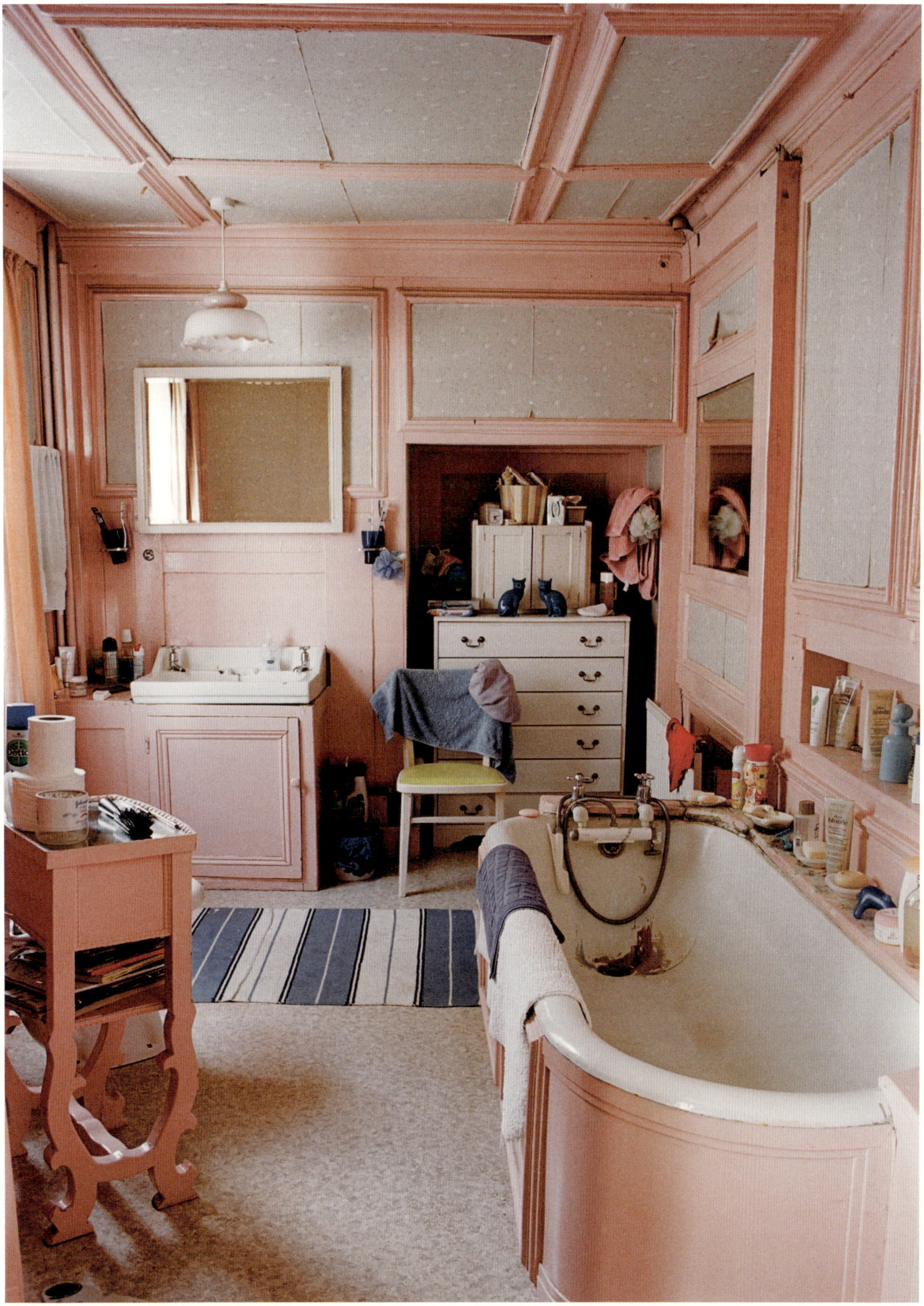
blonde
blonde

Granny or Grandmamma?
Nanny or Nan?
Grandma or Grandmother?
Nana or Gran?

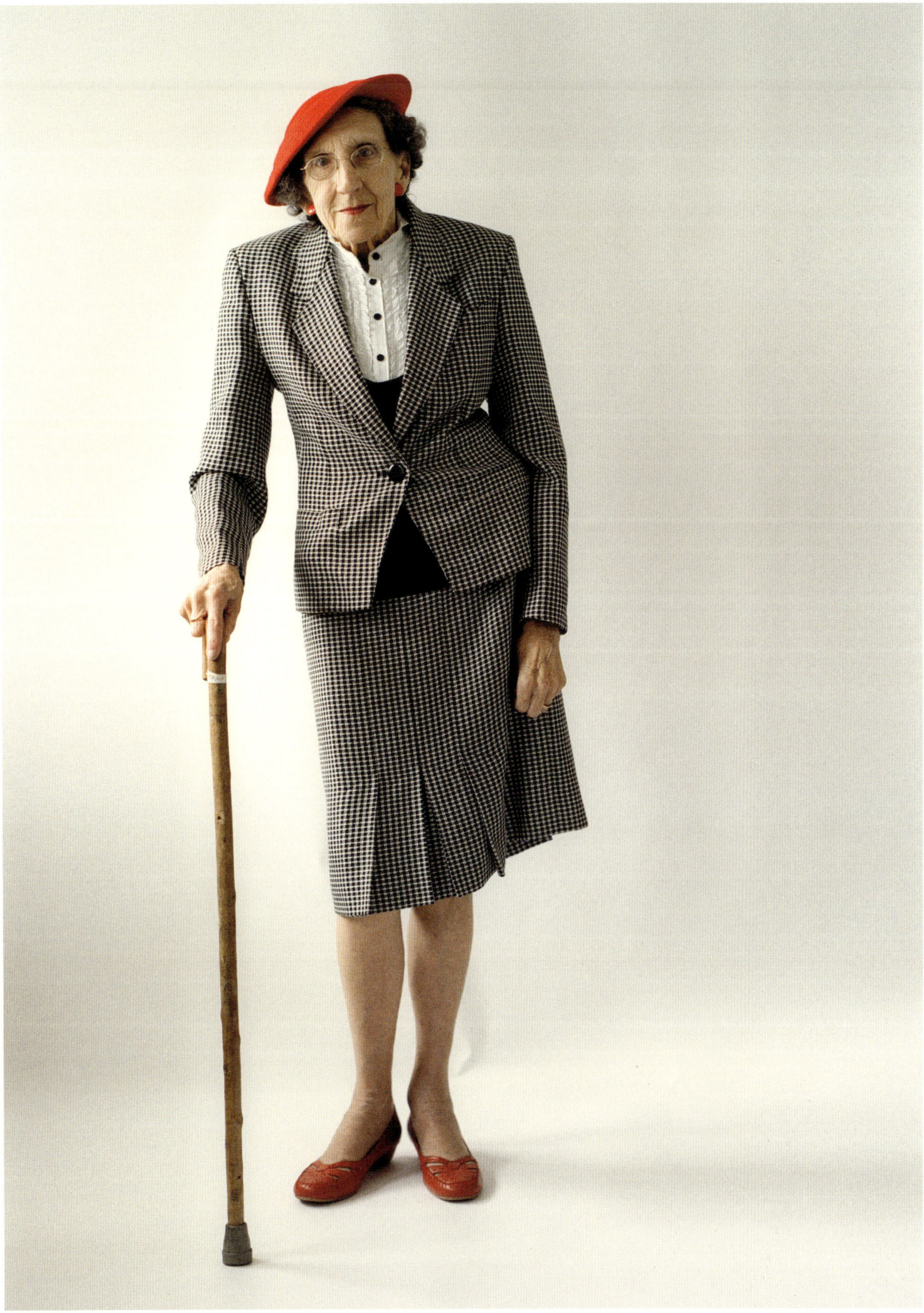

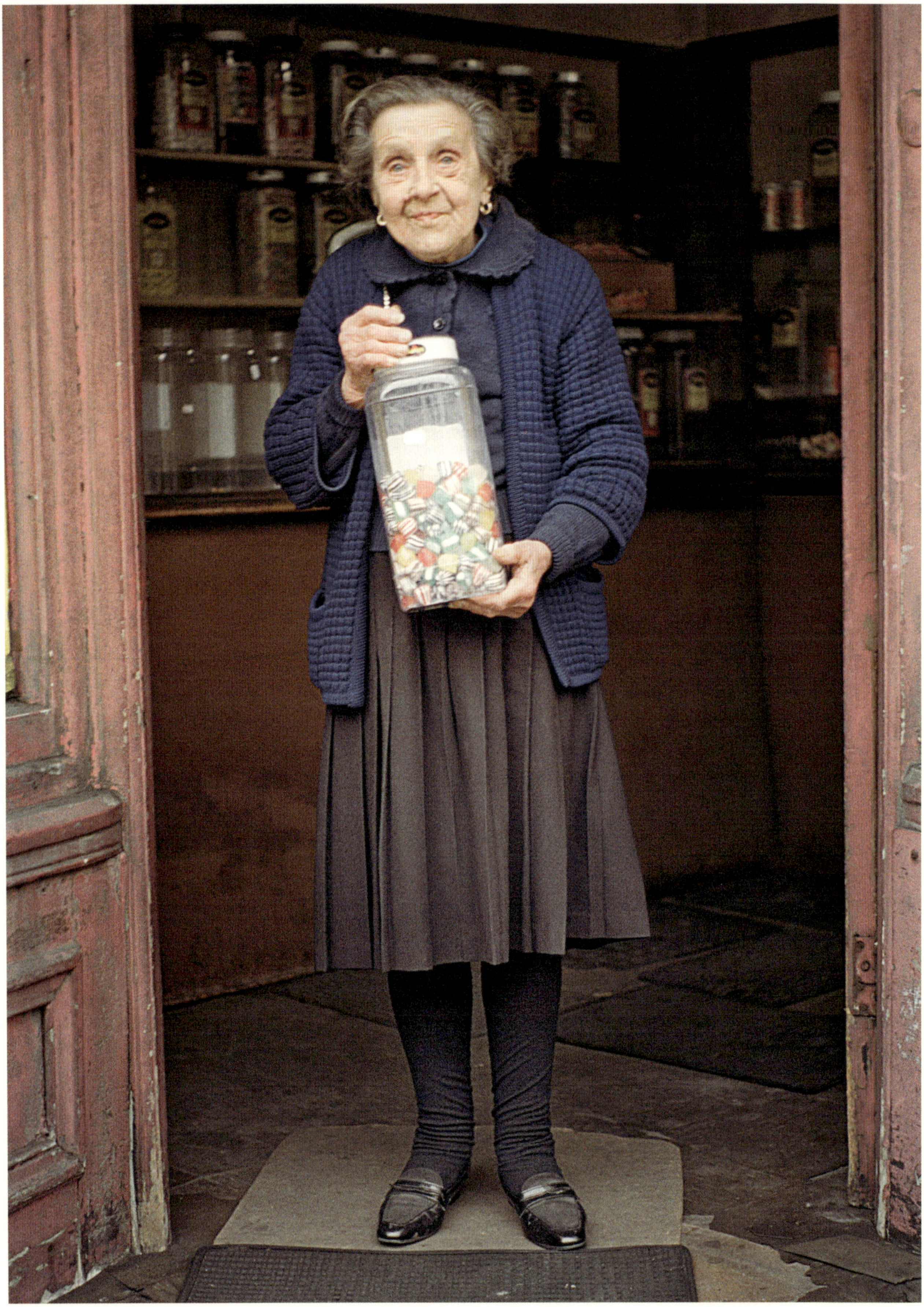

H

Hattie takes her humbug jar
From her highest shelf.
'Have you been a helpful child?
Then help yourself!'

I

I spy with my little eye,
Isn't that Ivy inching by?

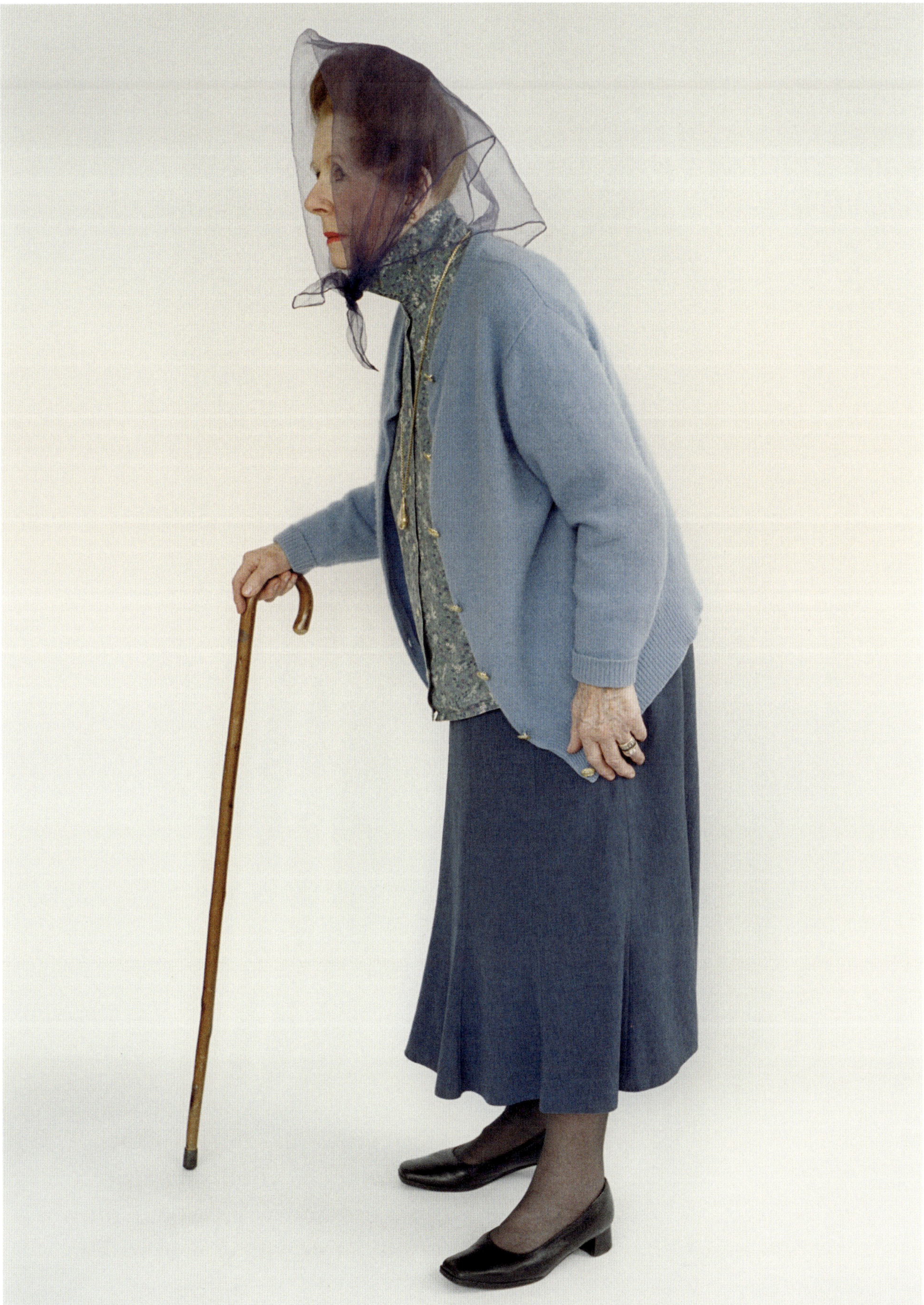

J

Joyce is a senior citizen now,
Yet she enjoyed youthful glories.
Jog Joyce's memory, and you'll allow
Joyce has some jolly good stories.

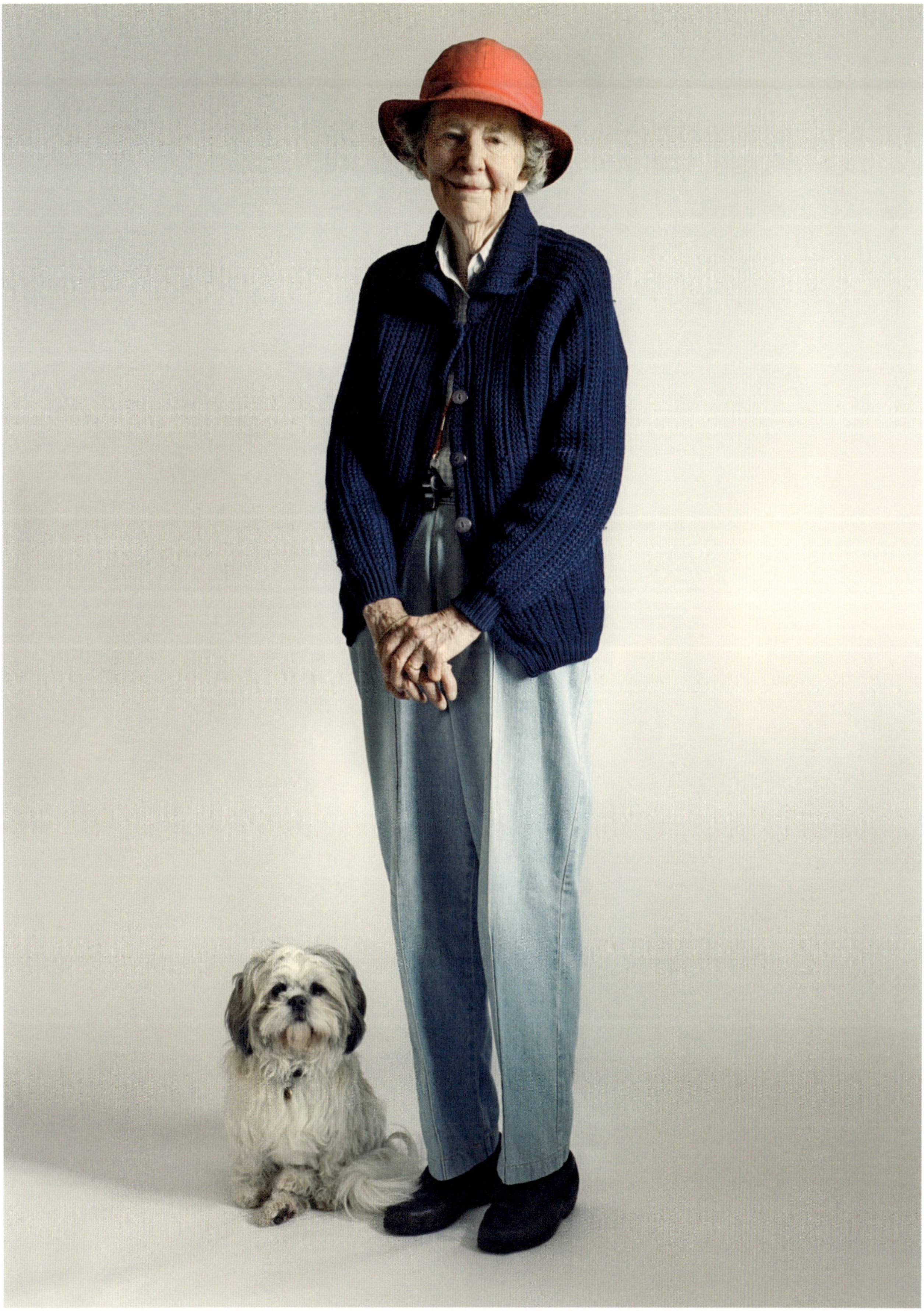

K

Kitty Knight is keen on knitting.
Kitty knits an awful lot.
Did she knit that kilt she's wearing?
I think knot.

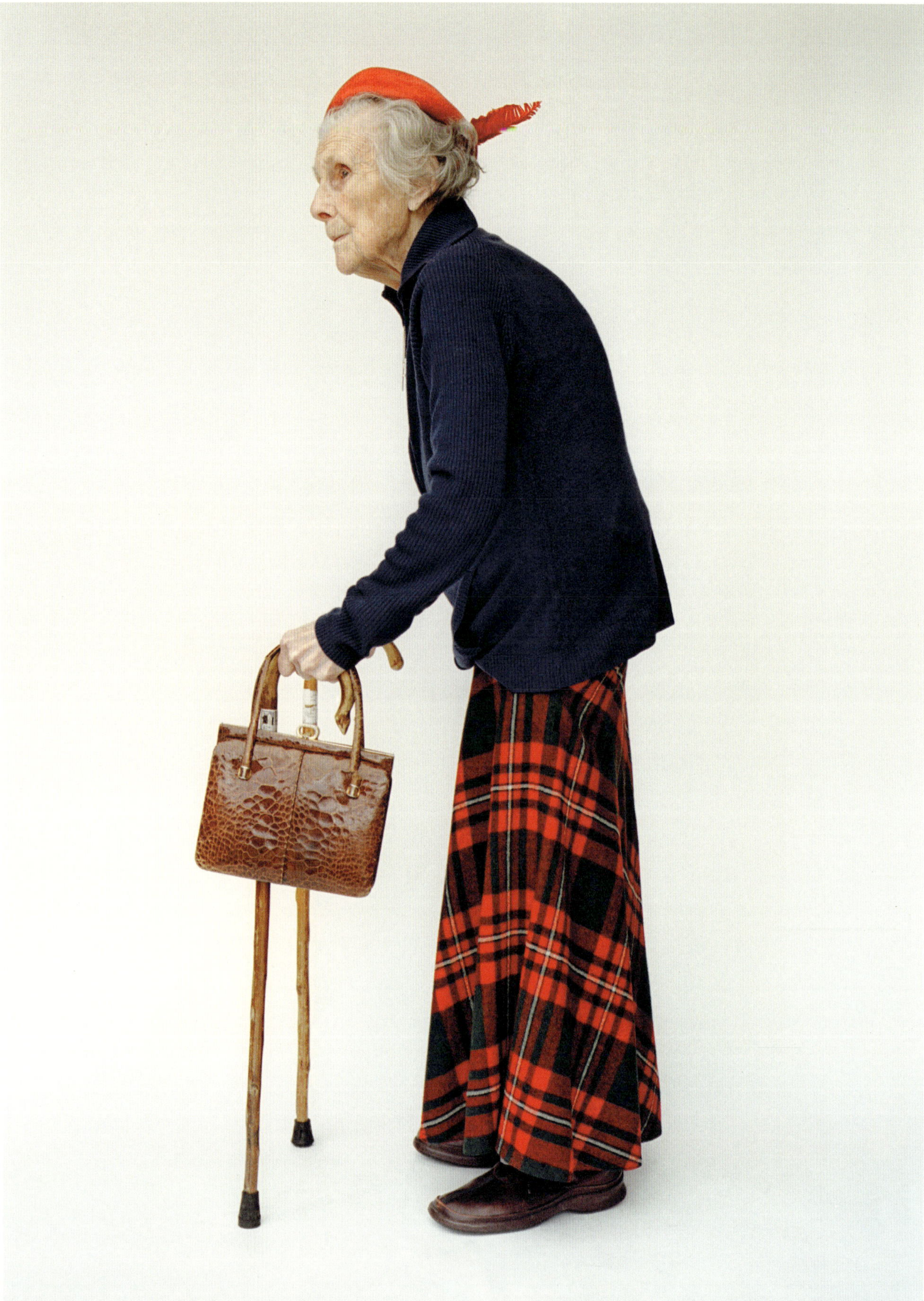

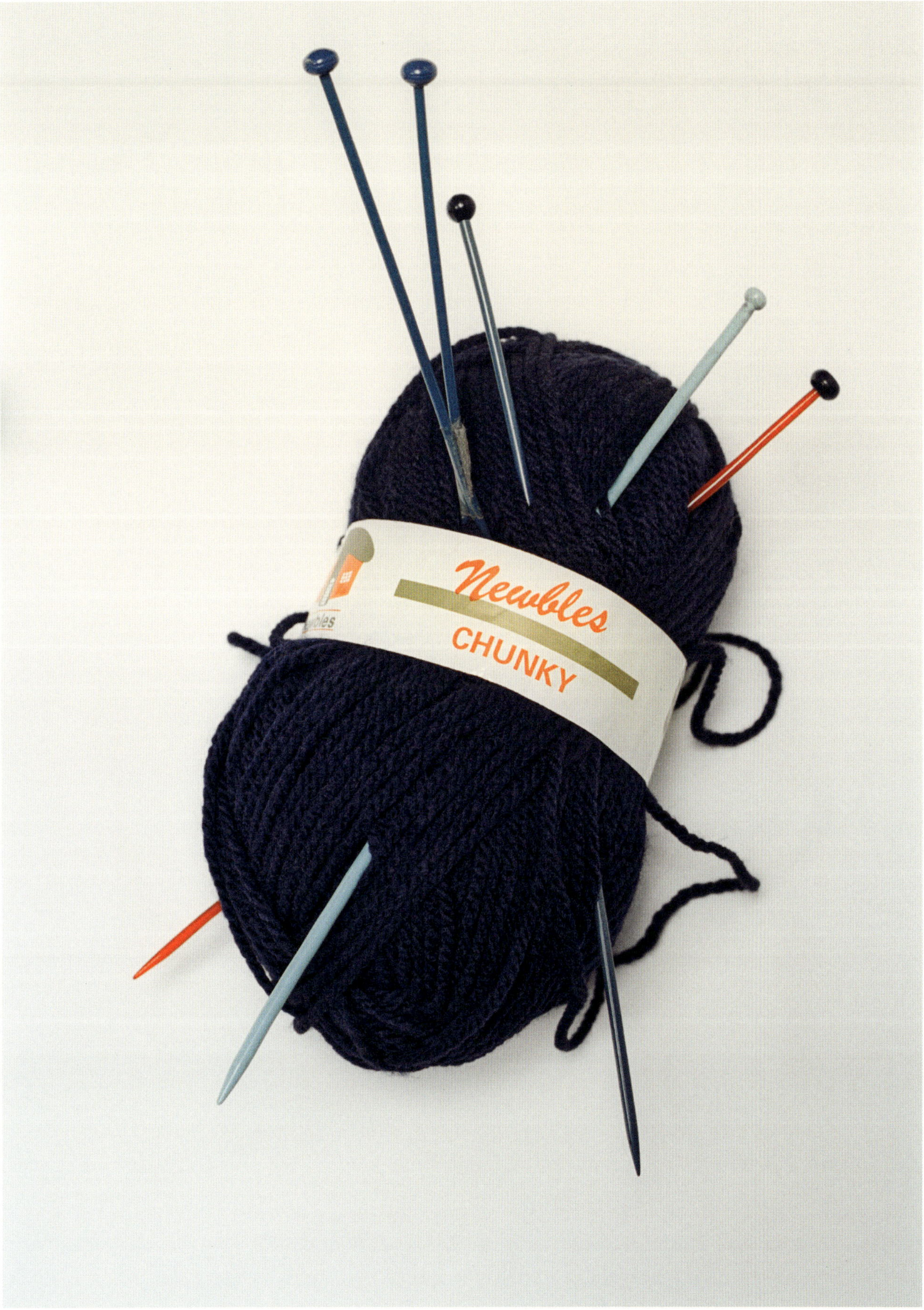

Newbles
CHUNKY

L

Lucinda was alas averse
To exercise of any sort.
Lucinda's legs are now a curse;
Poor Lucinda needs support.
Guard against such future loss,
Do not try and dodge lacrosse.

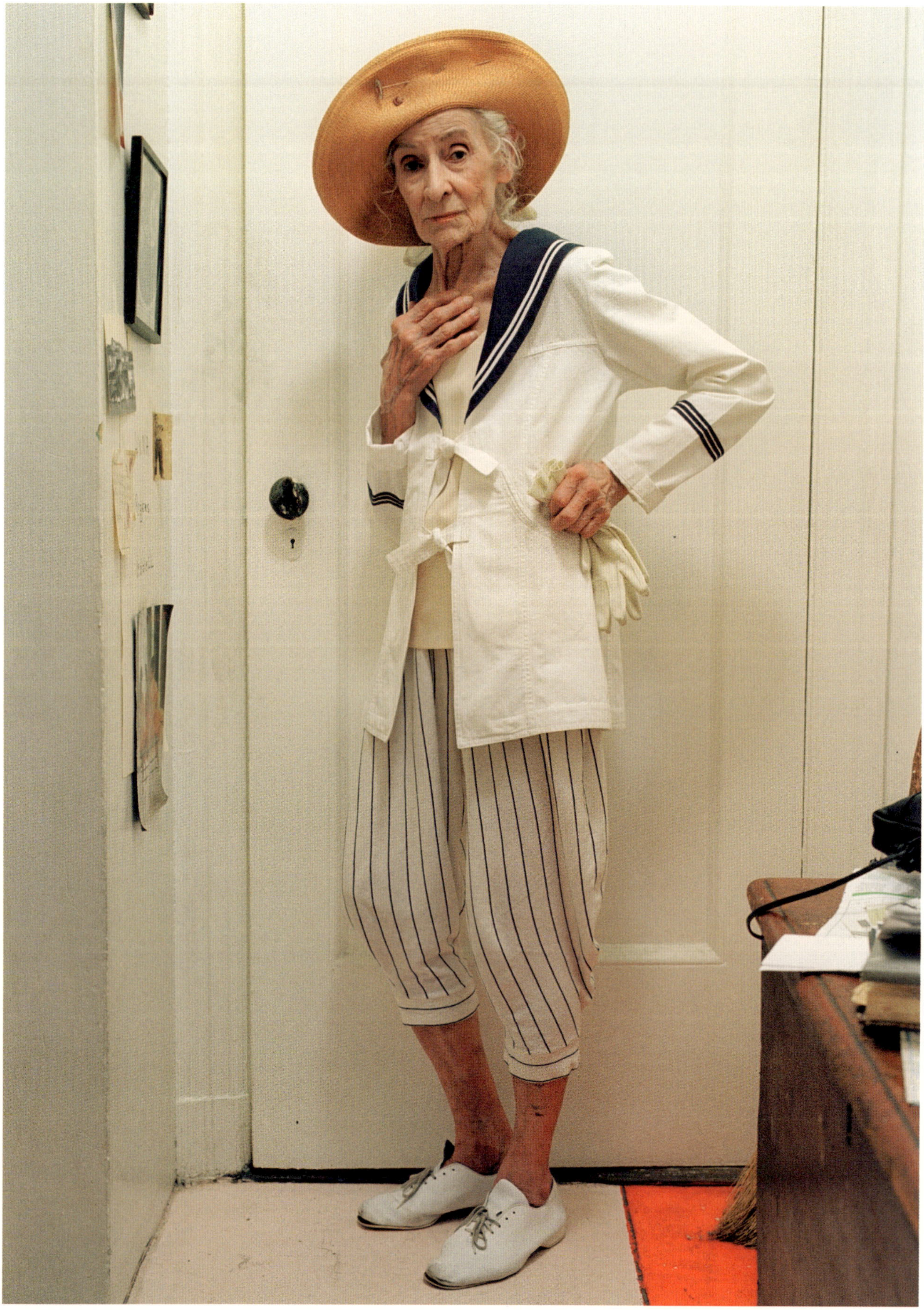

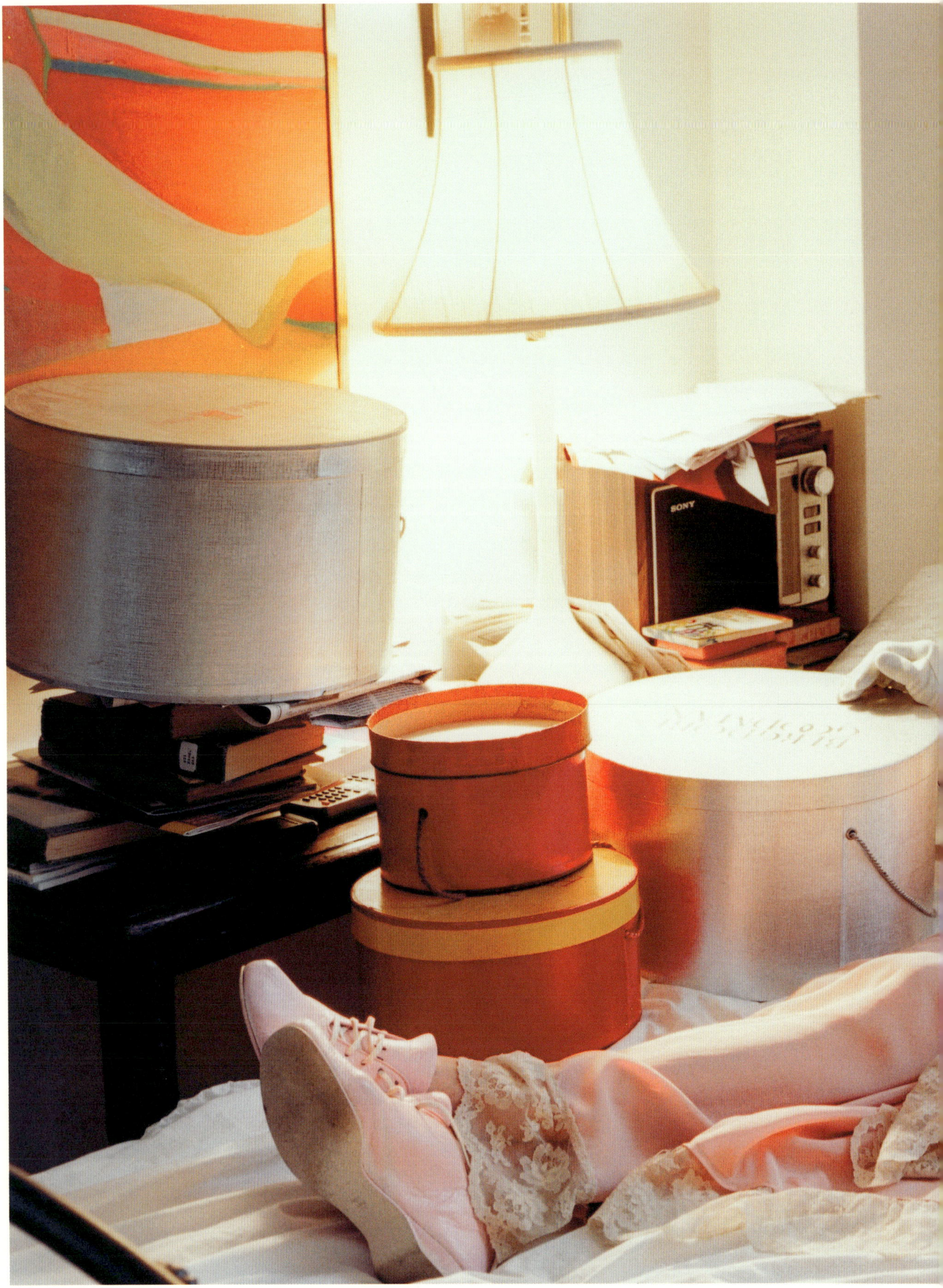
SONY

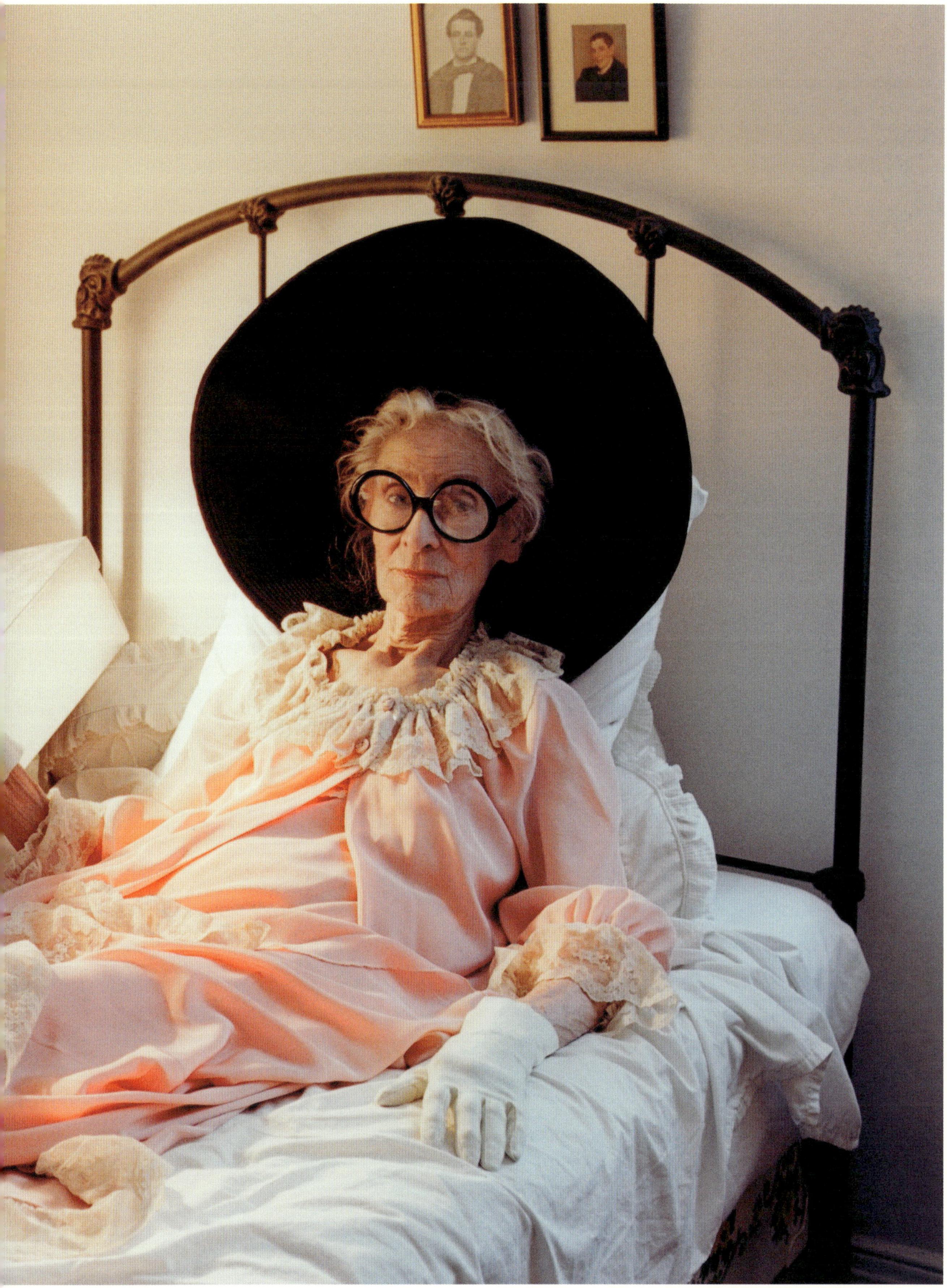

M

Mona measures models
With her measuring tape.
They moan worse than Mona
And struggle to escape.
However, Mona always wins.
(She's armed, you see, with pins.)

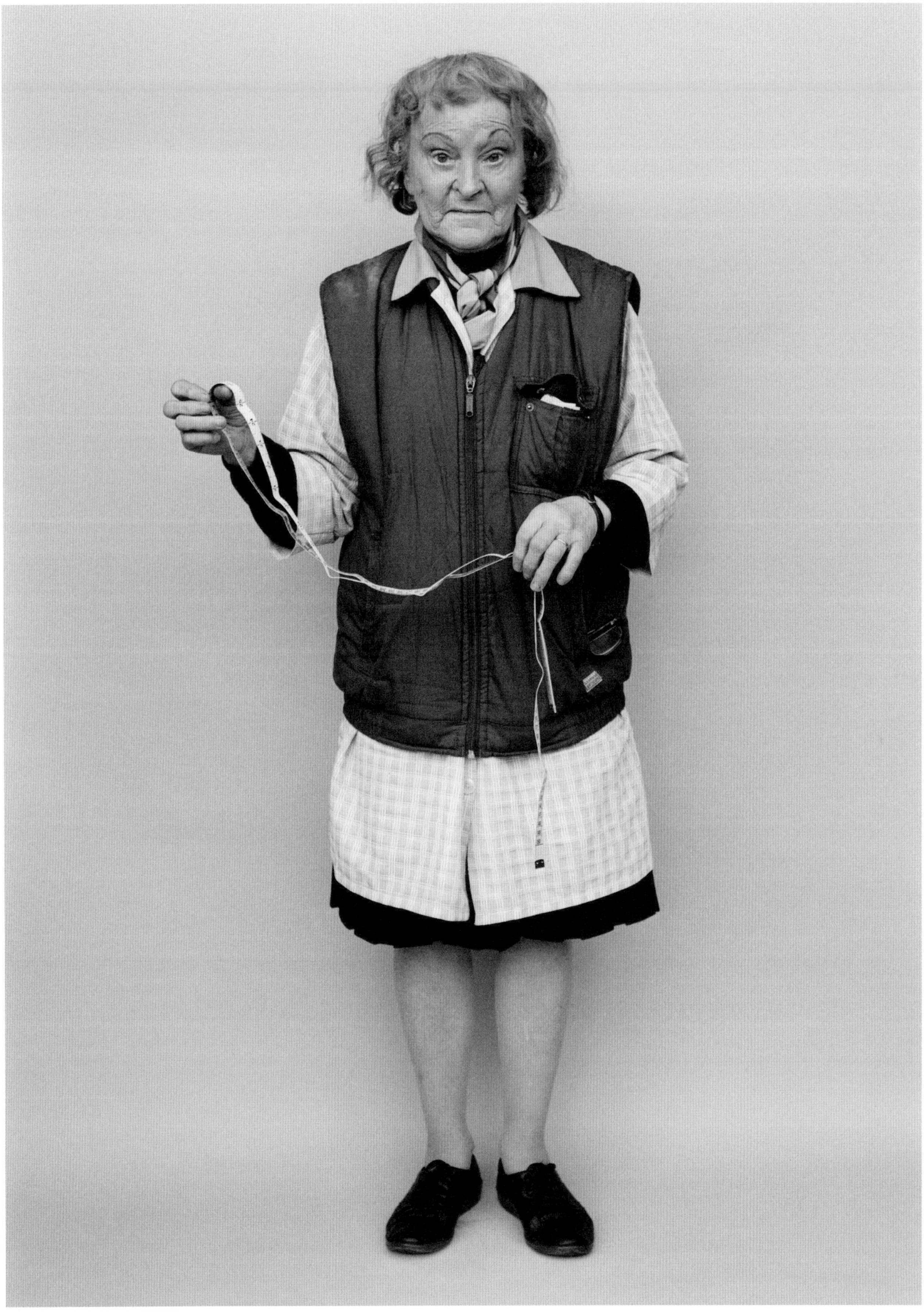

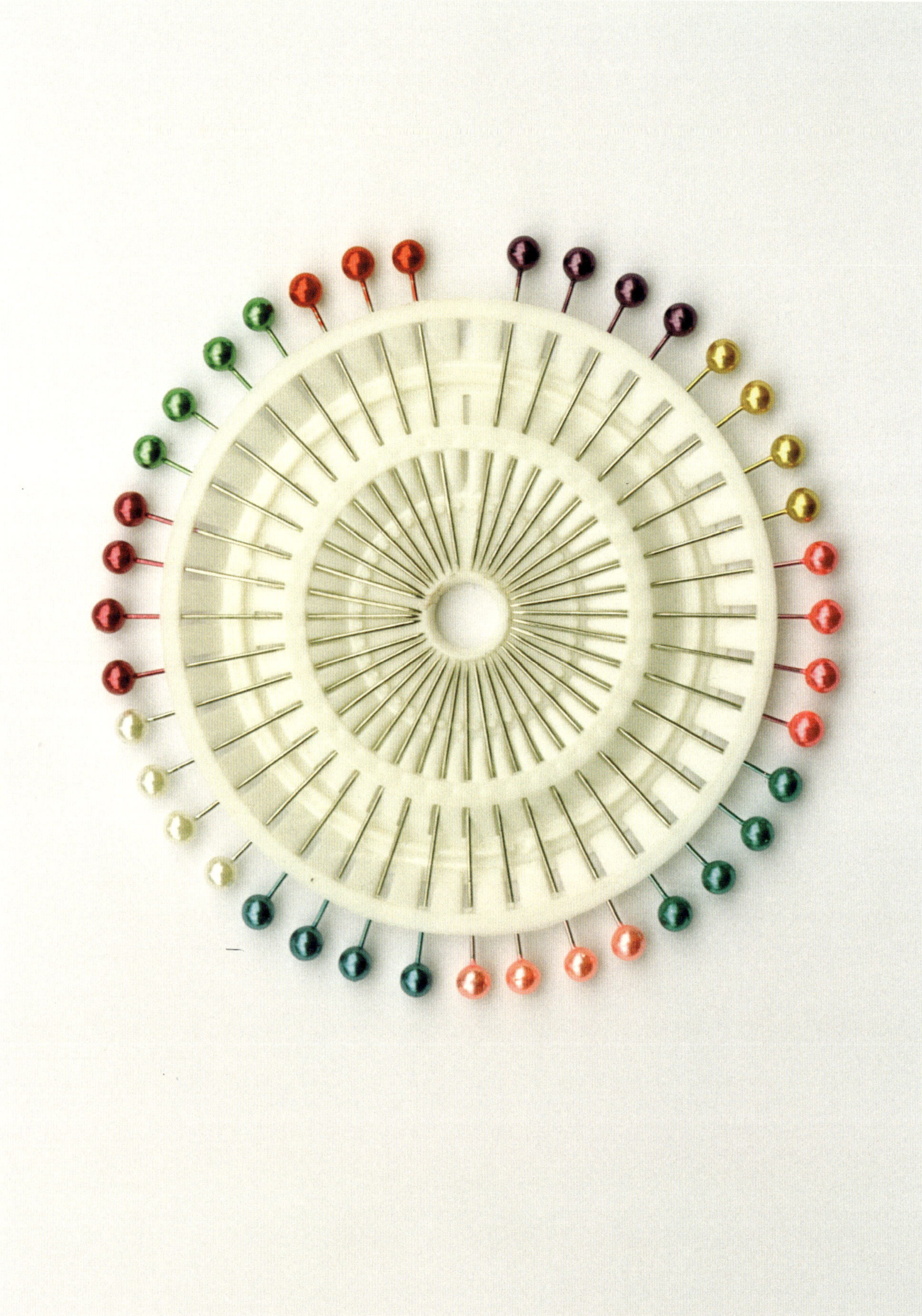

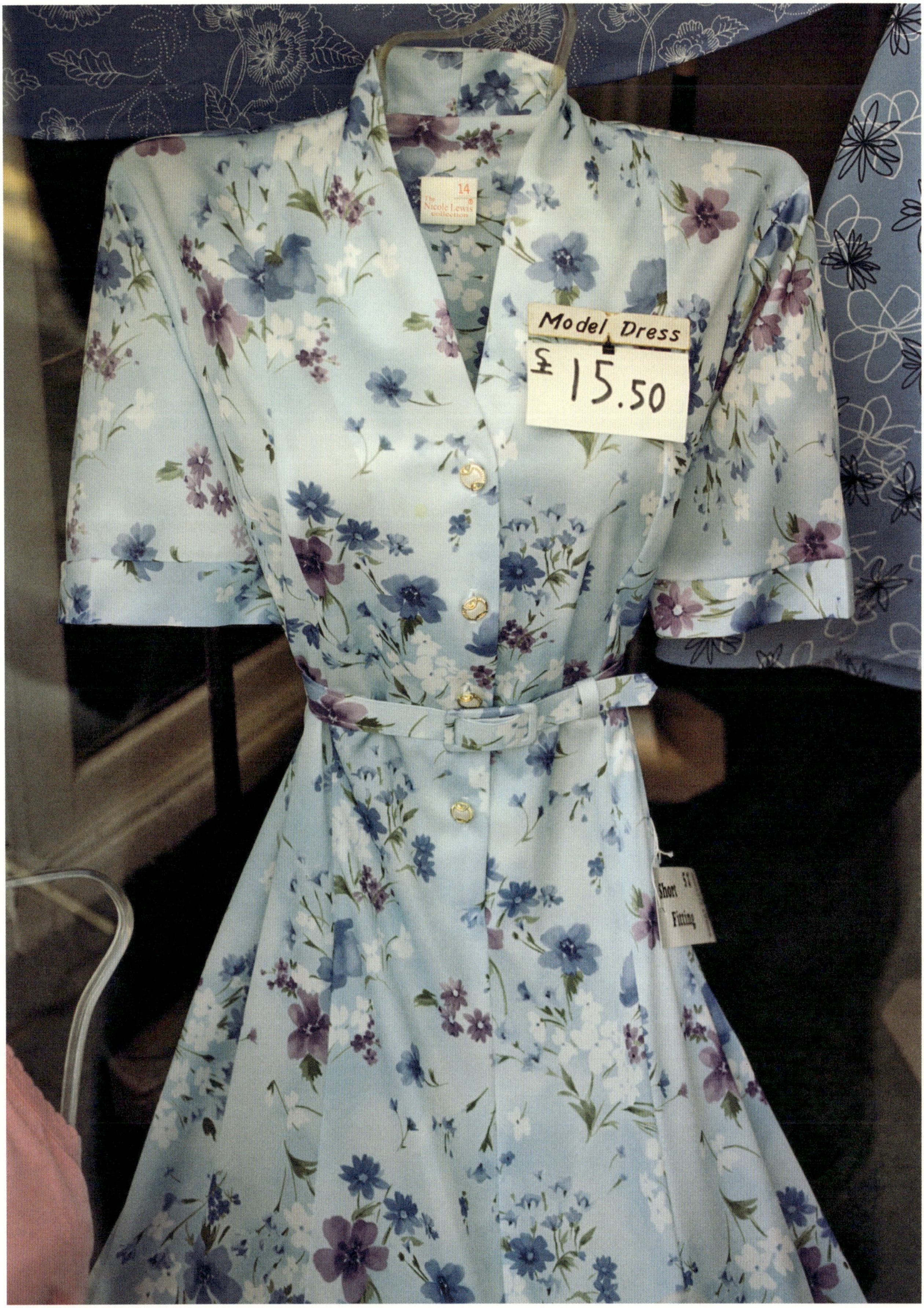
14
The Nicole Lewis collection
Model Dress
£15.50
Short
Fitting

N

Nasturtiums, narcissi and nectarines too,
Gardeners never have nothing to do.
Nadia is busier than she can mention
(Gardens, like Grannies, need constant attention).

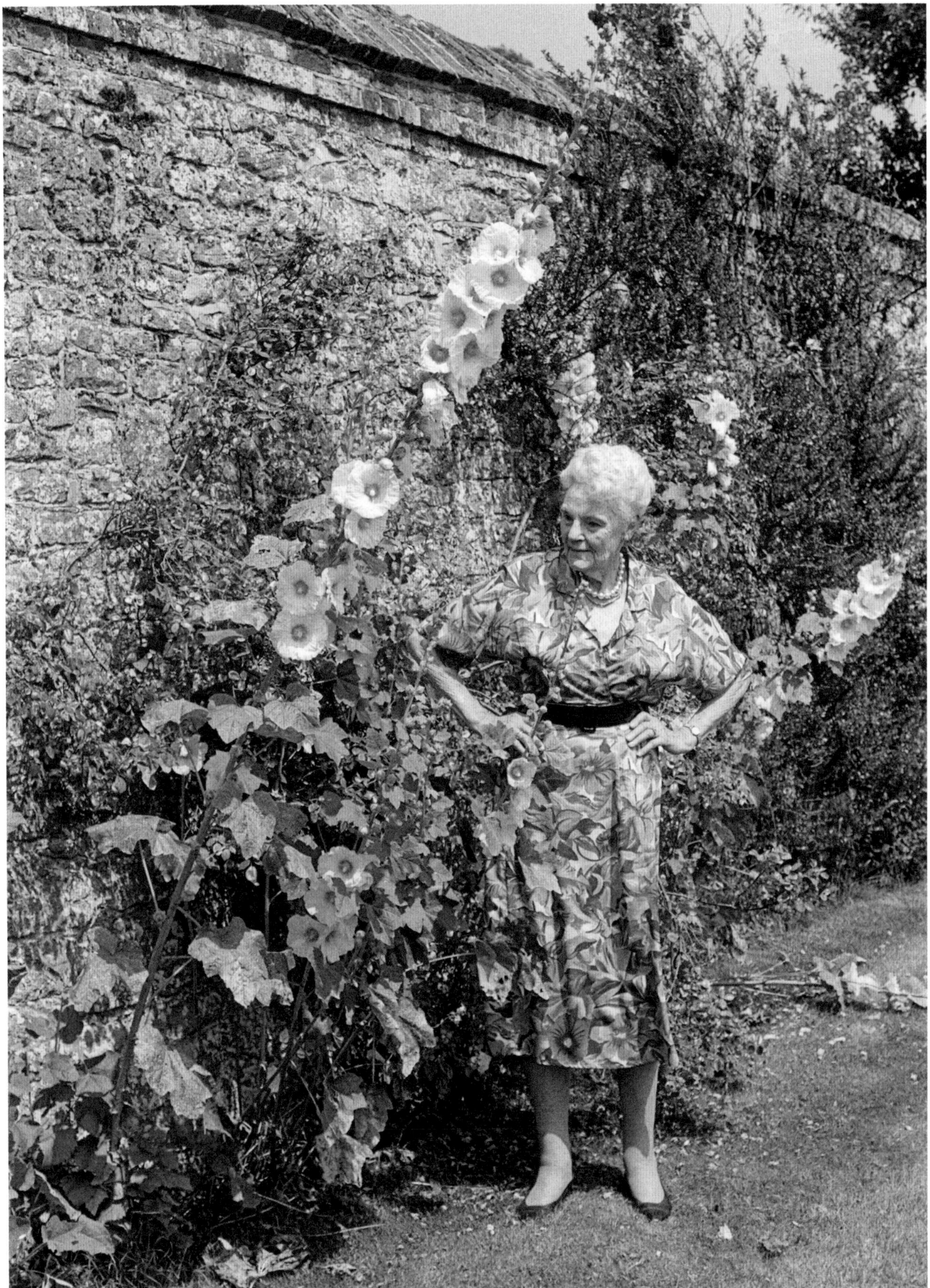

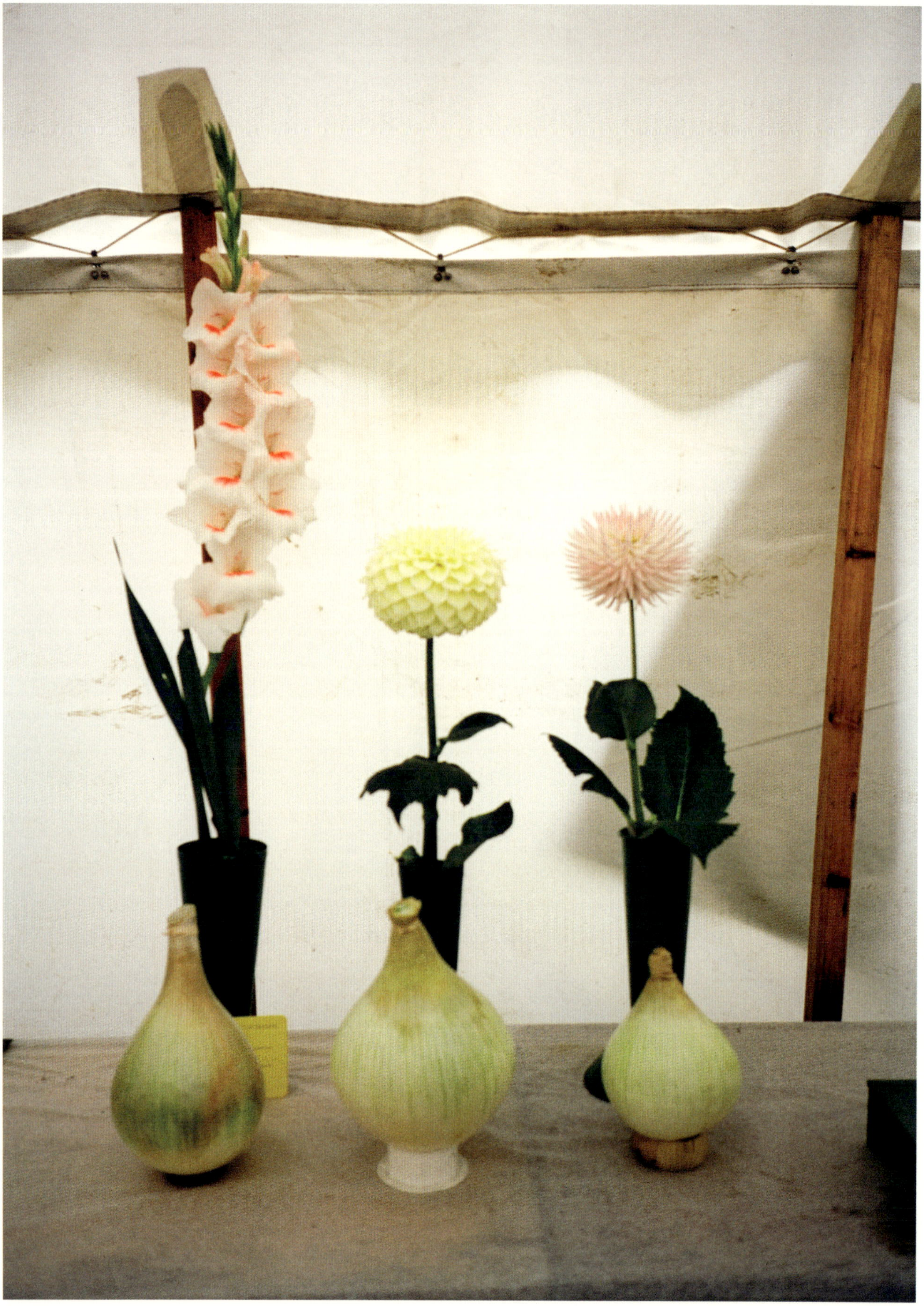

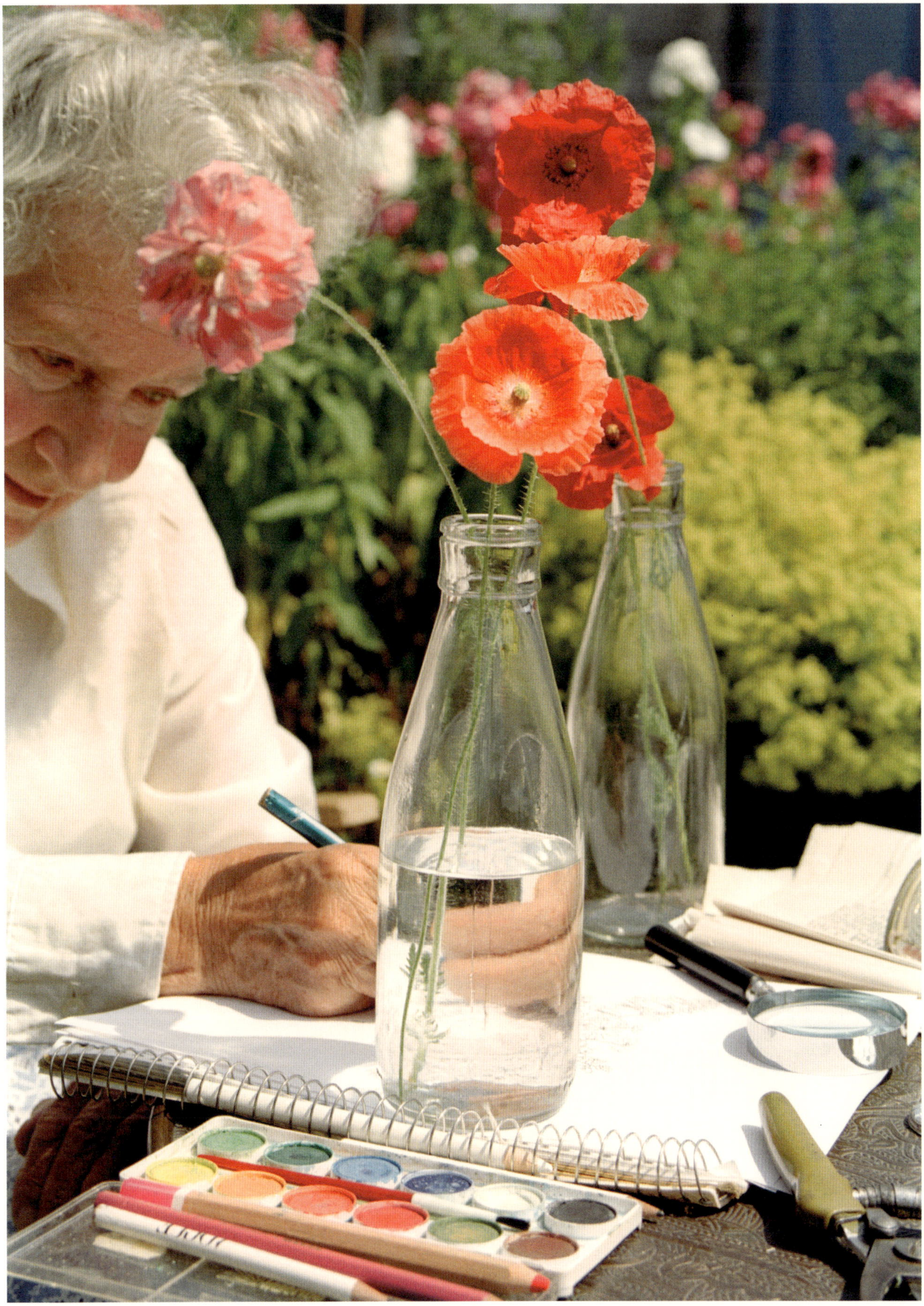

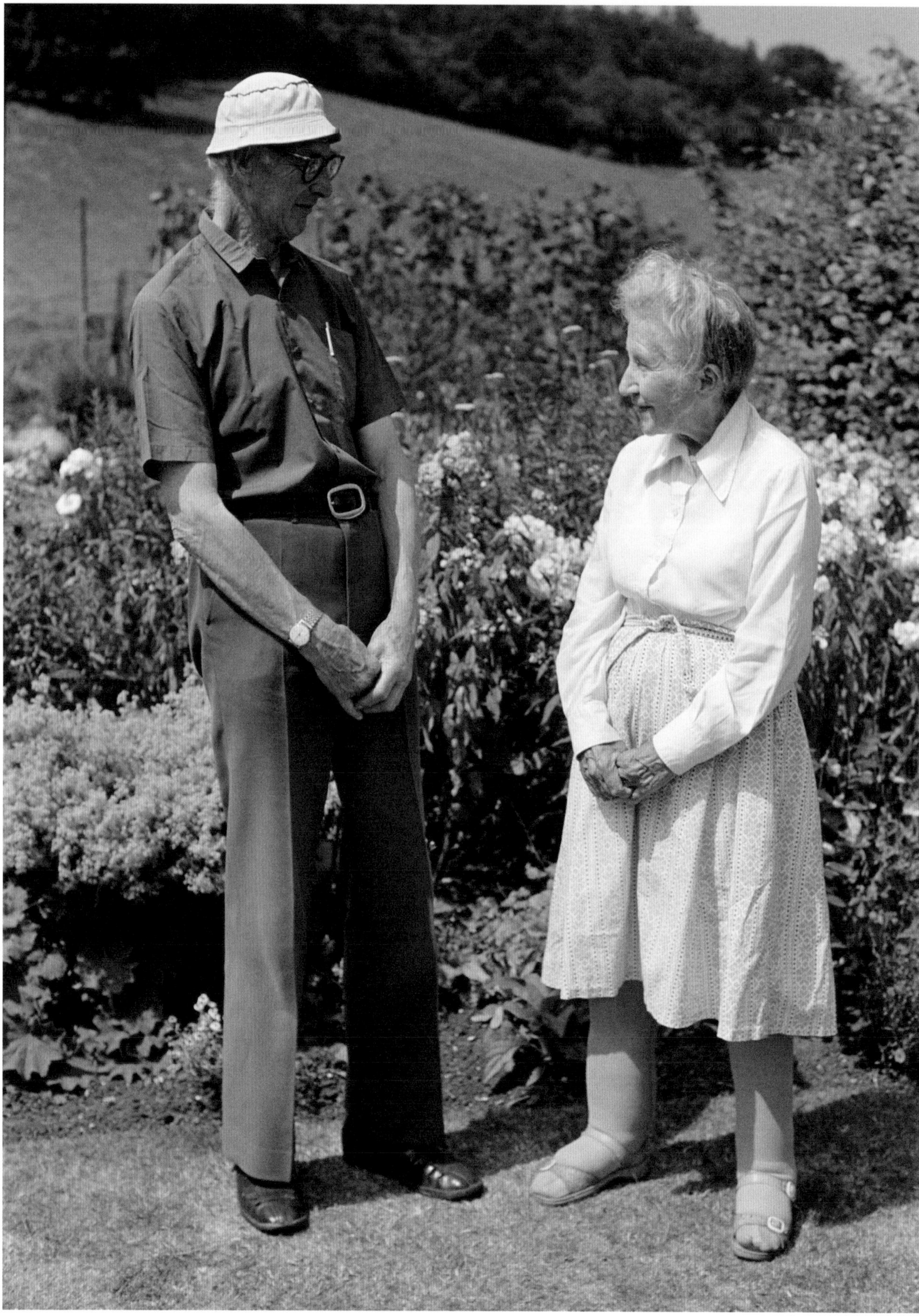

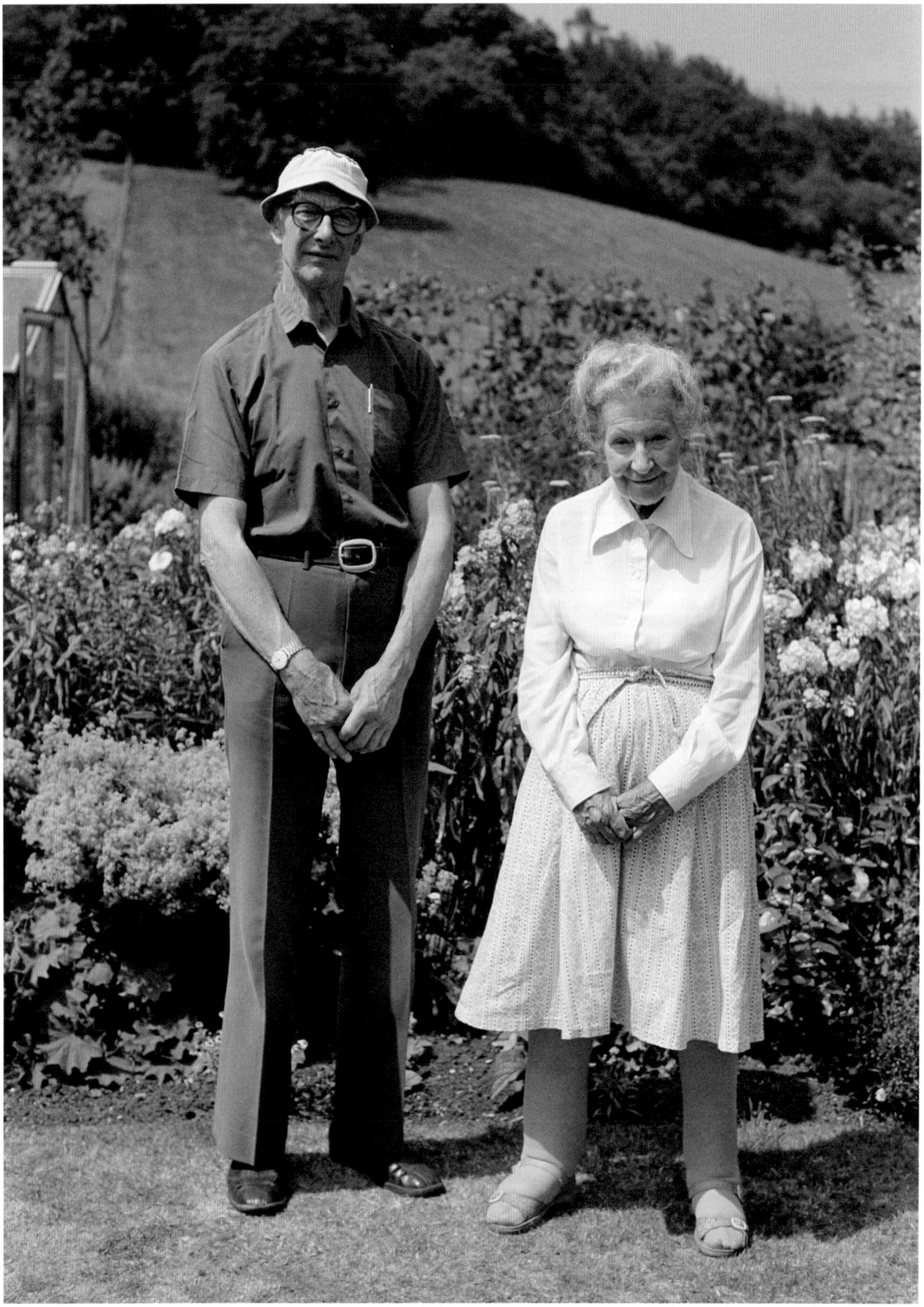

O

Olive may be older now,
But Olive loves a show.
'Onward and upward,'
Olive says, 'Let's go!'

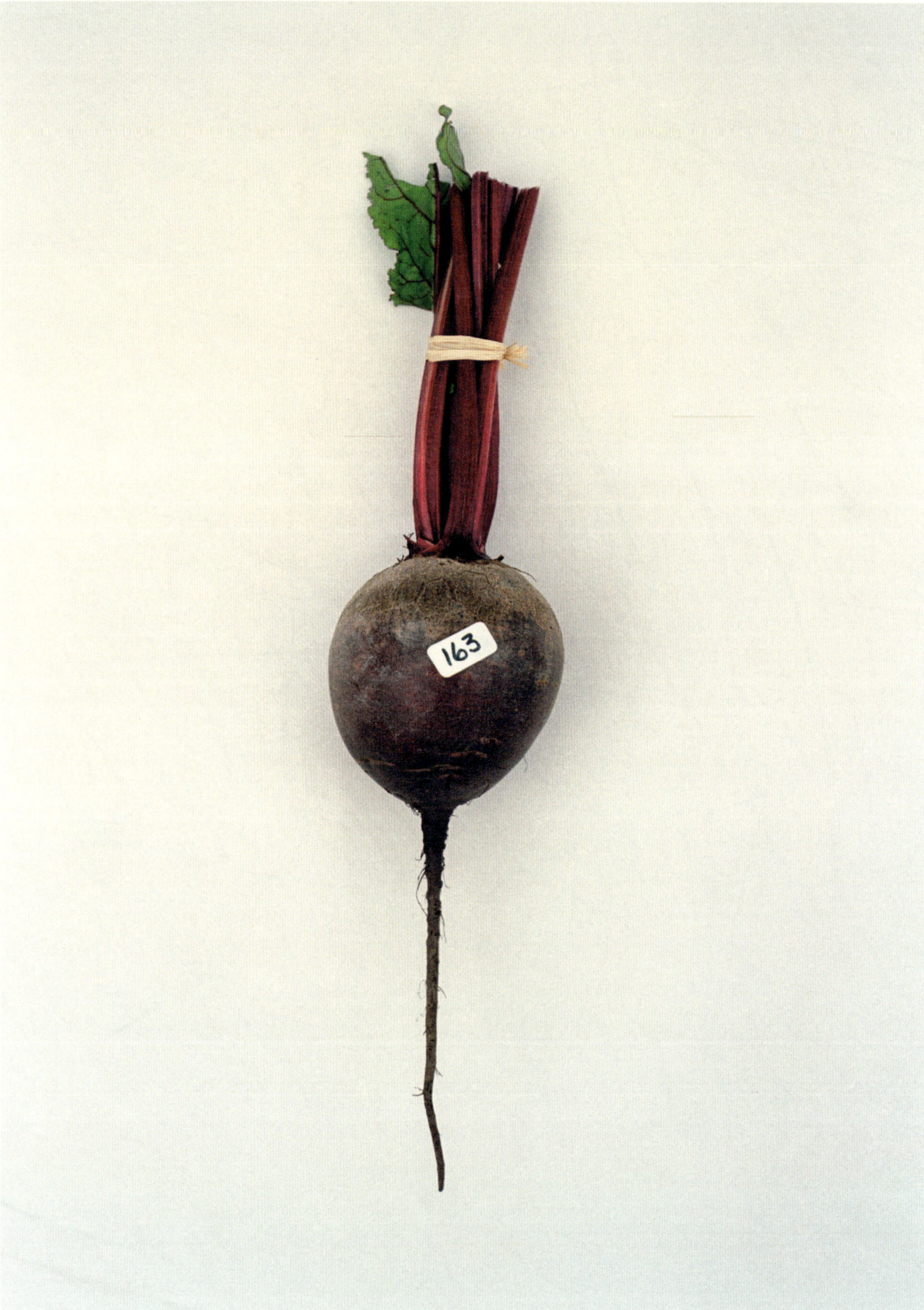
163

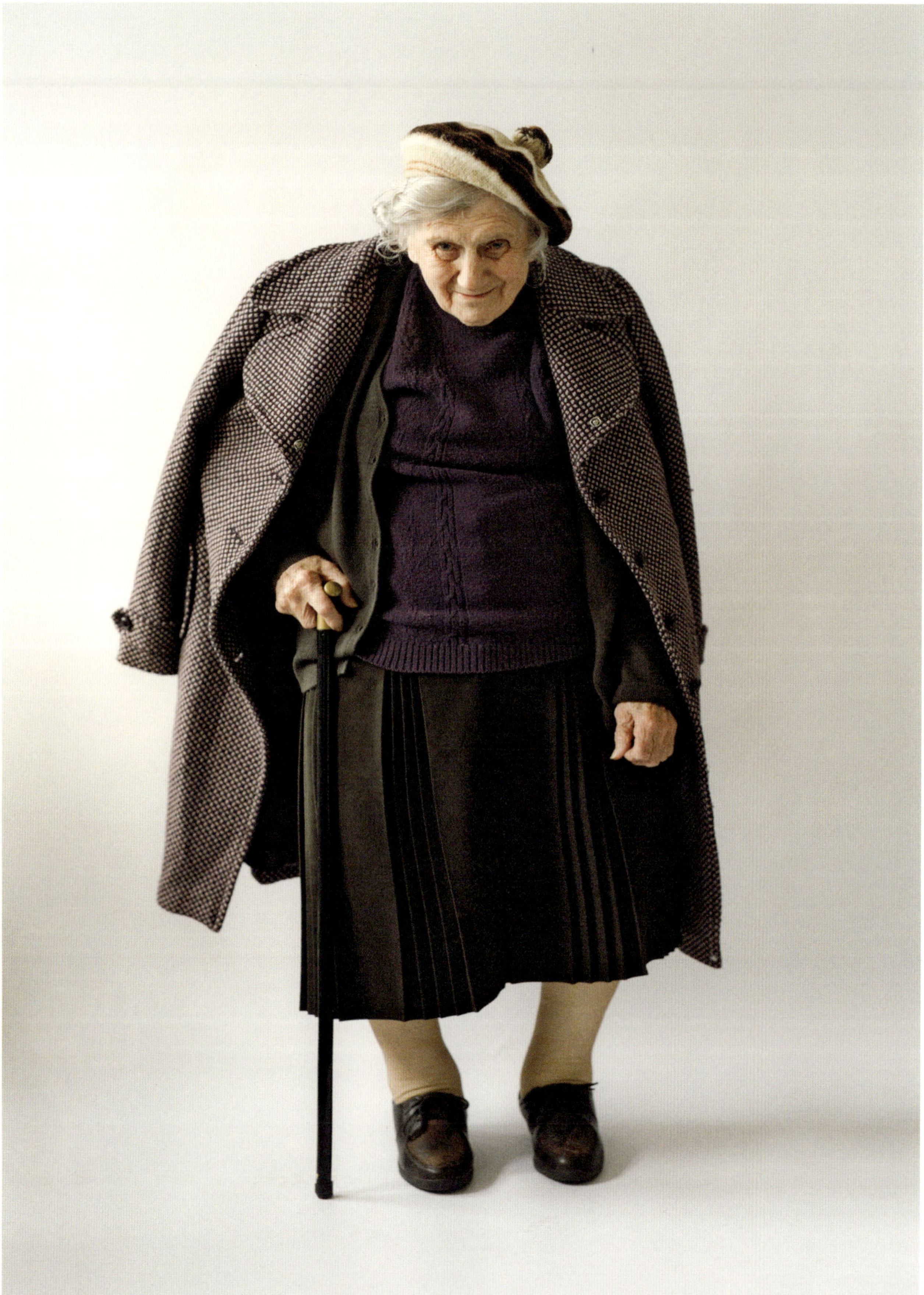

P

Patricia poses with panache.
The puma coat is fake.
The pearls, I'd say, are perfect,
The platforms, a mistake.

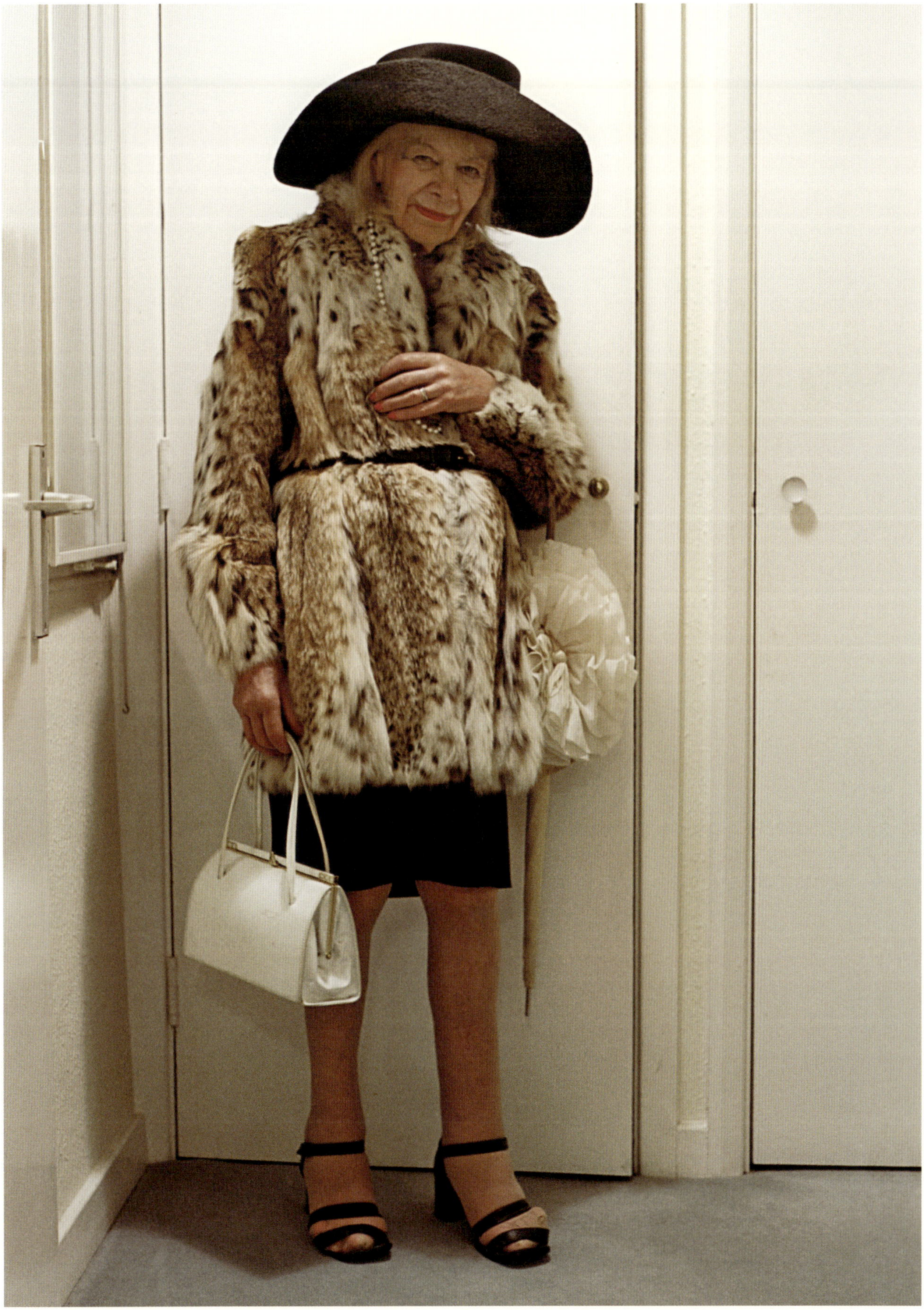

Queenie holds old-fashioned views.
Better mind your Ps and Qs.

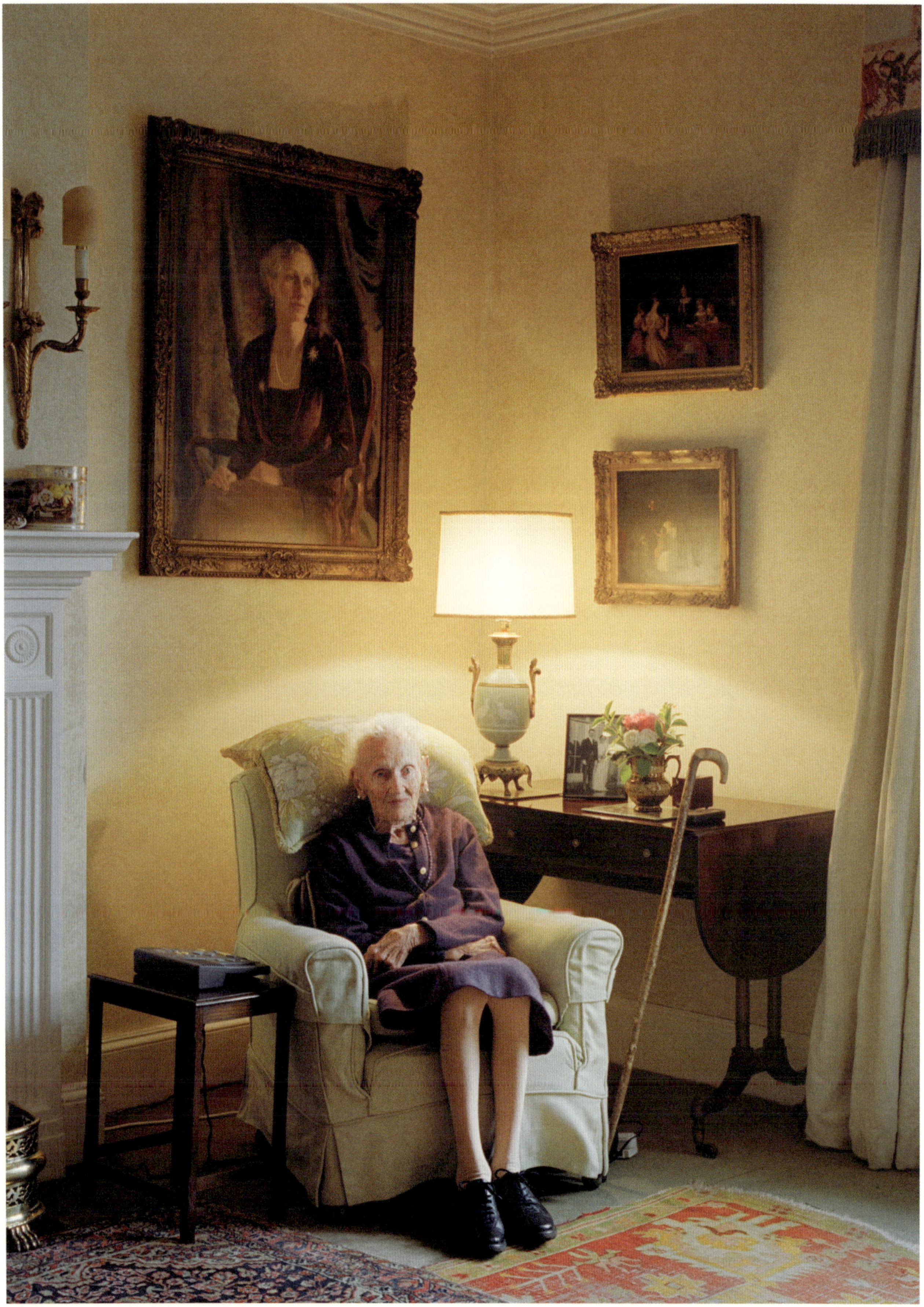

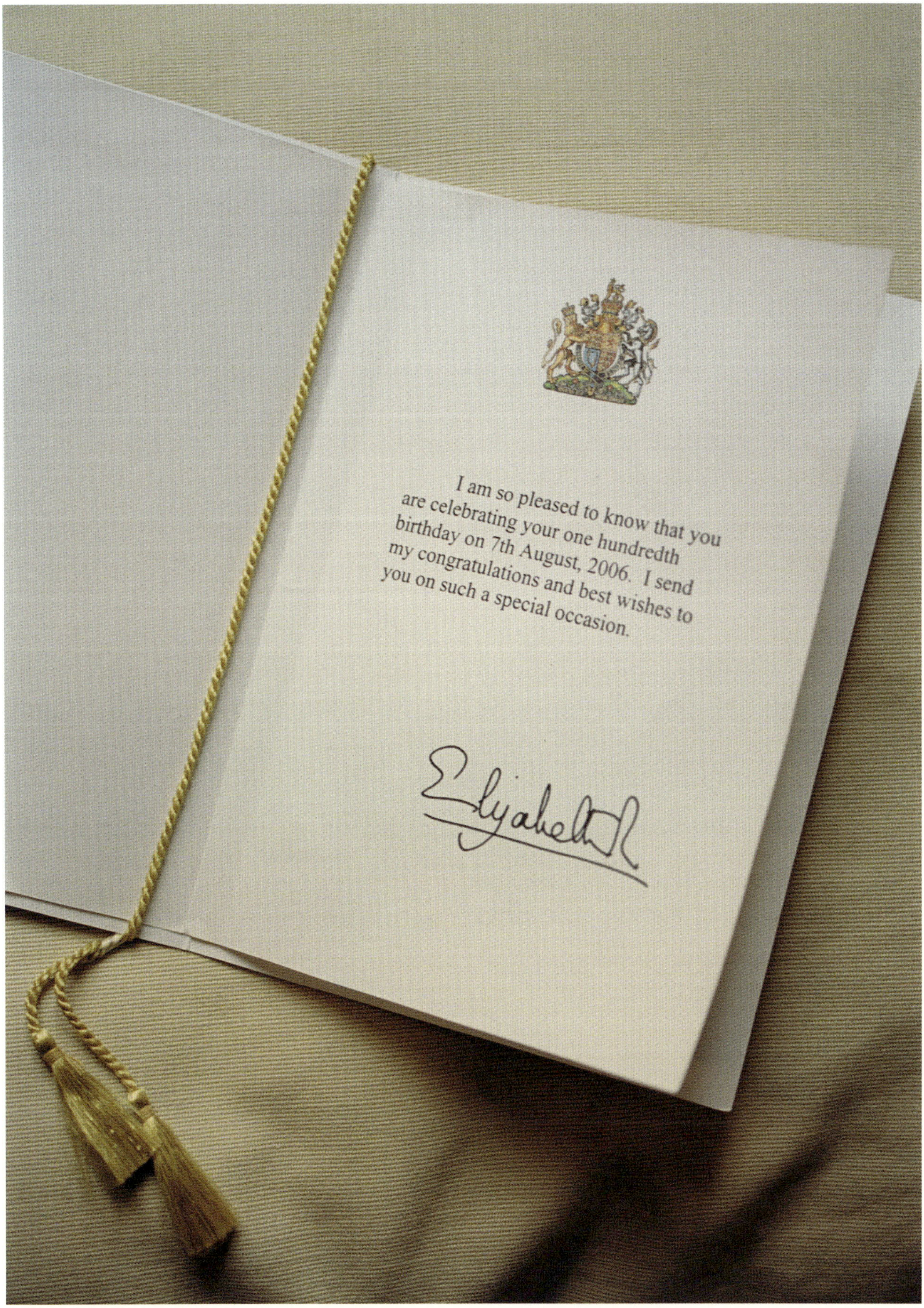
I am so pleased to know that you
are celebrating your one hundredth
birthday on 7th August, 2006. I send
my congratulations and best wishes to
you on such a special occasion.

R

Rosie's dog's called Rover.
(That's Rosie, bending over.)
She doesn't drive a Rover though,
She drives a Vauxhall Nova.

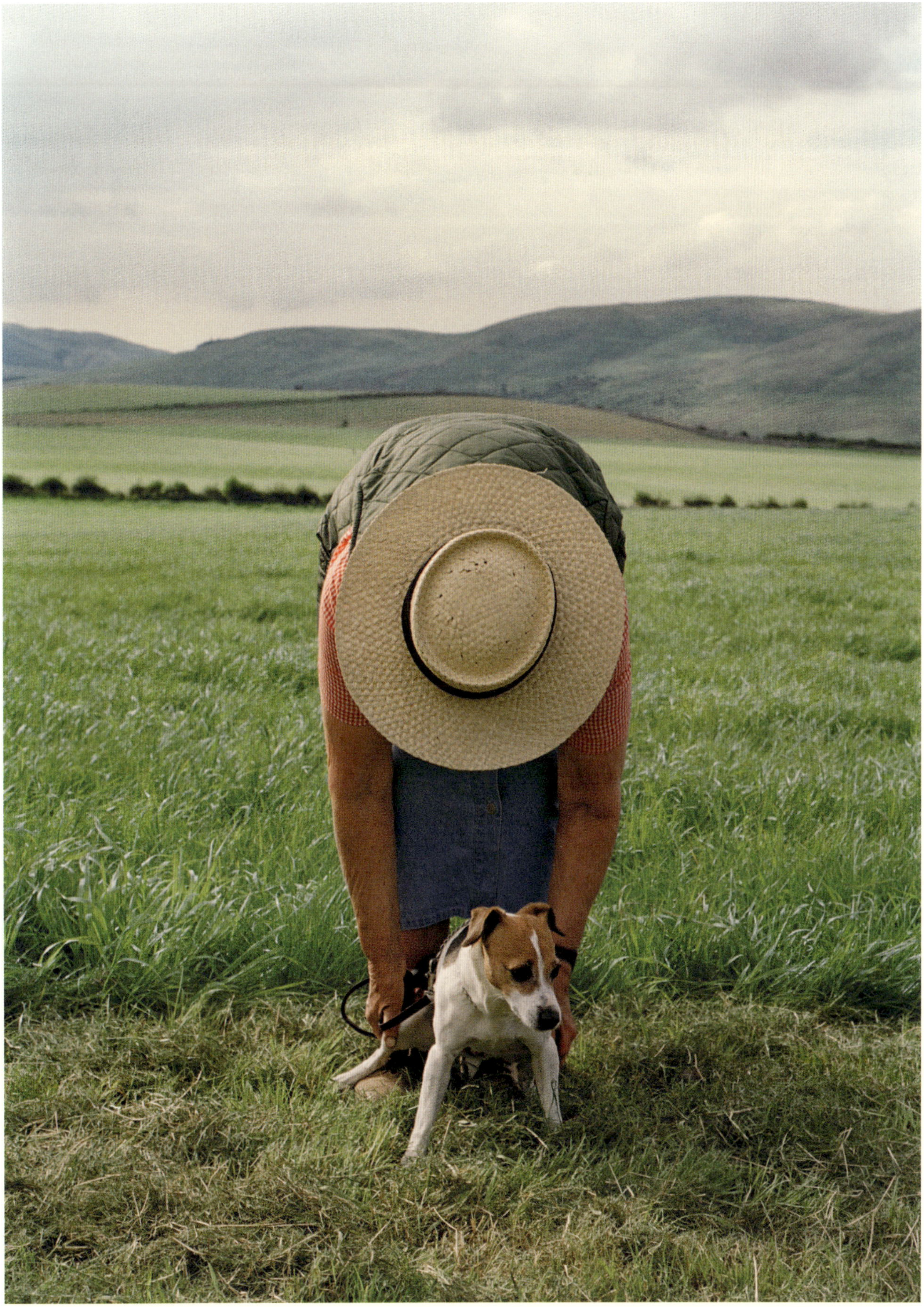

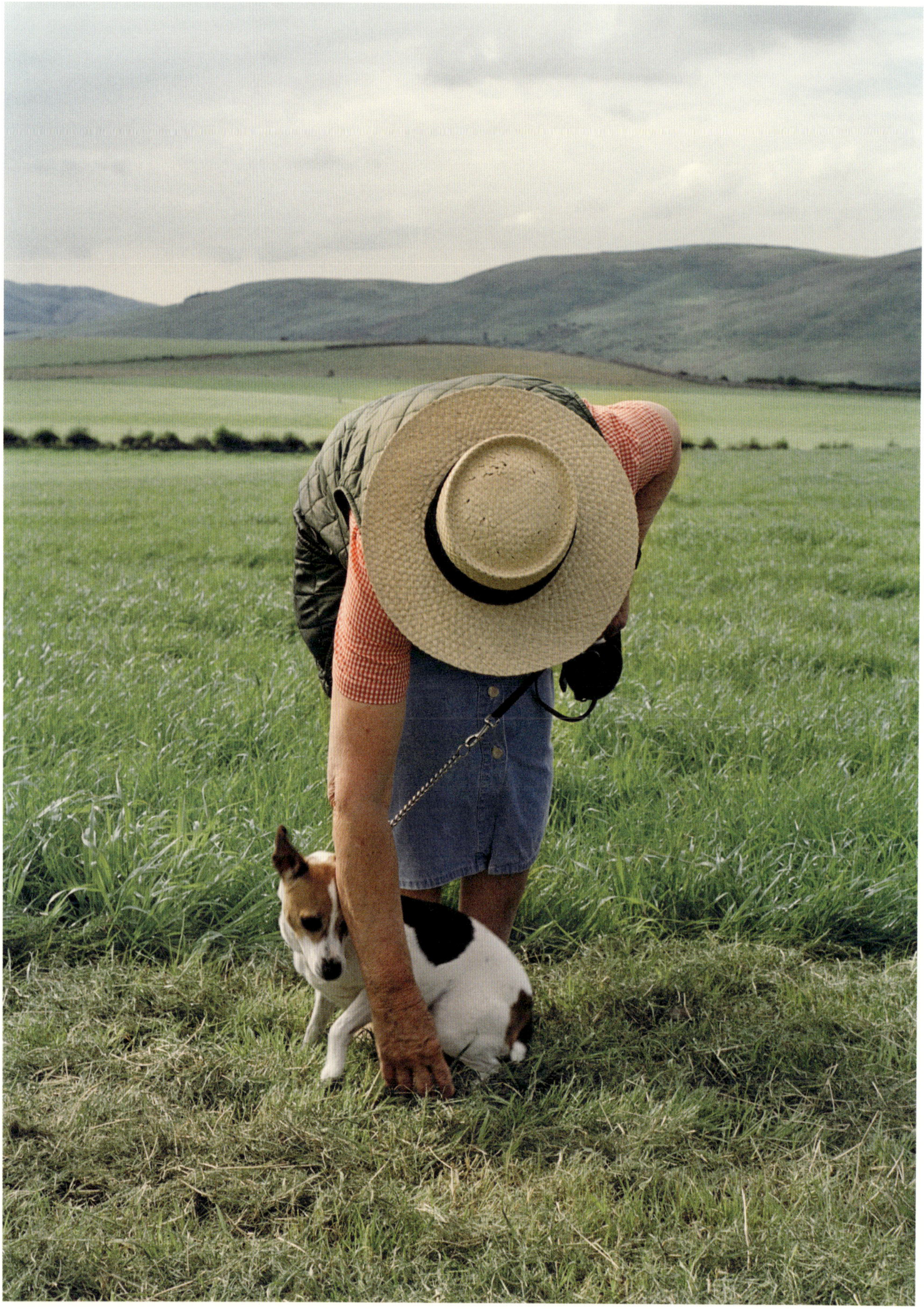

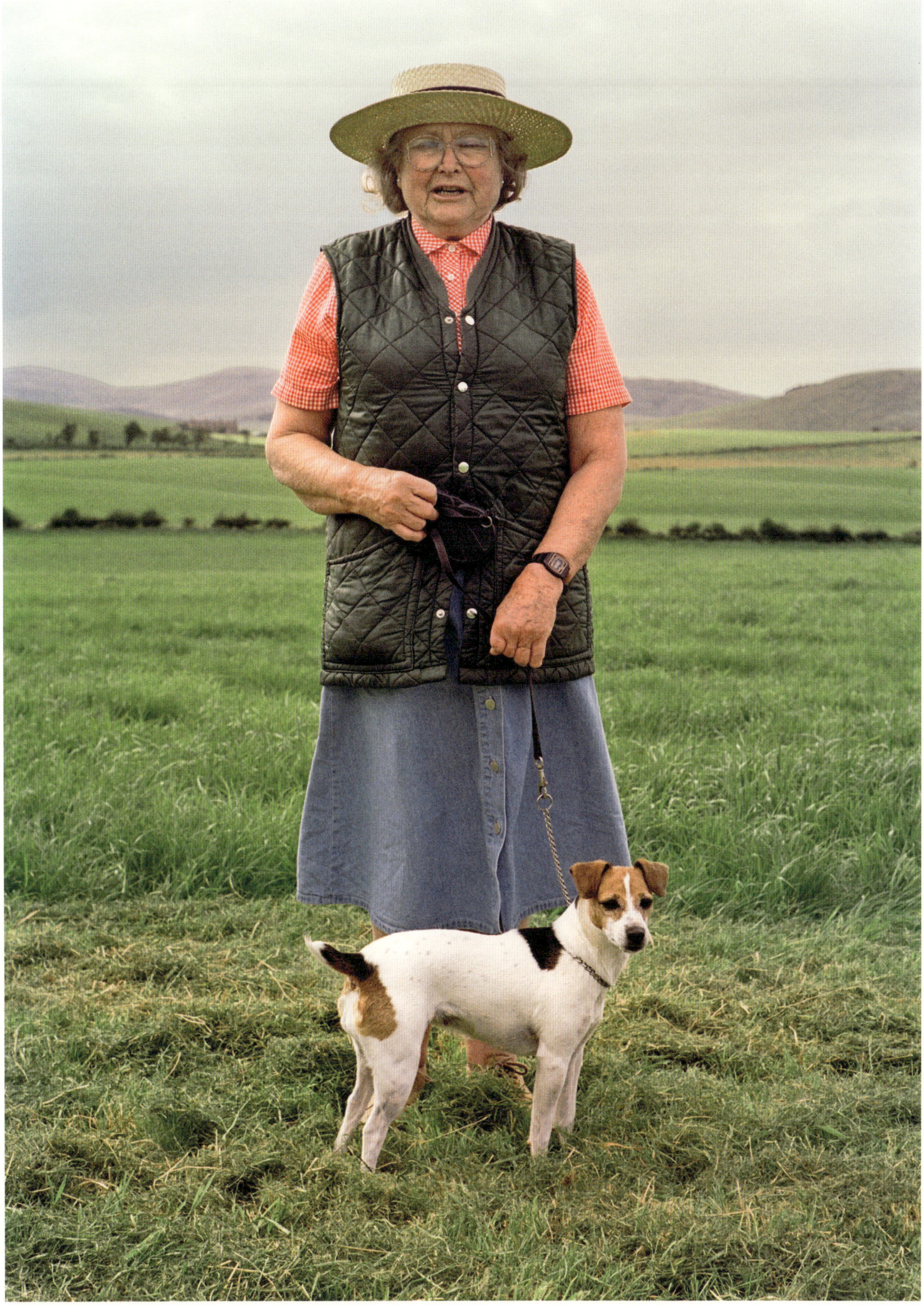

S

Sybil has
A stoutish stick
In case the going's tricky.
Go too quick
Without a stick
And things can get quite sticky.

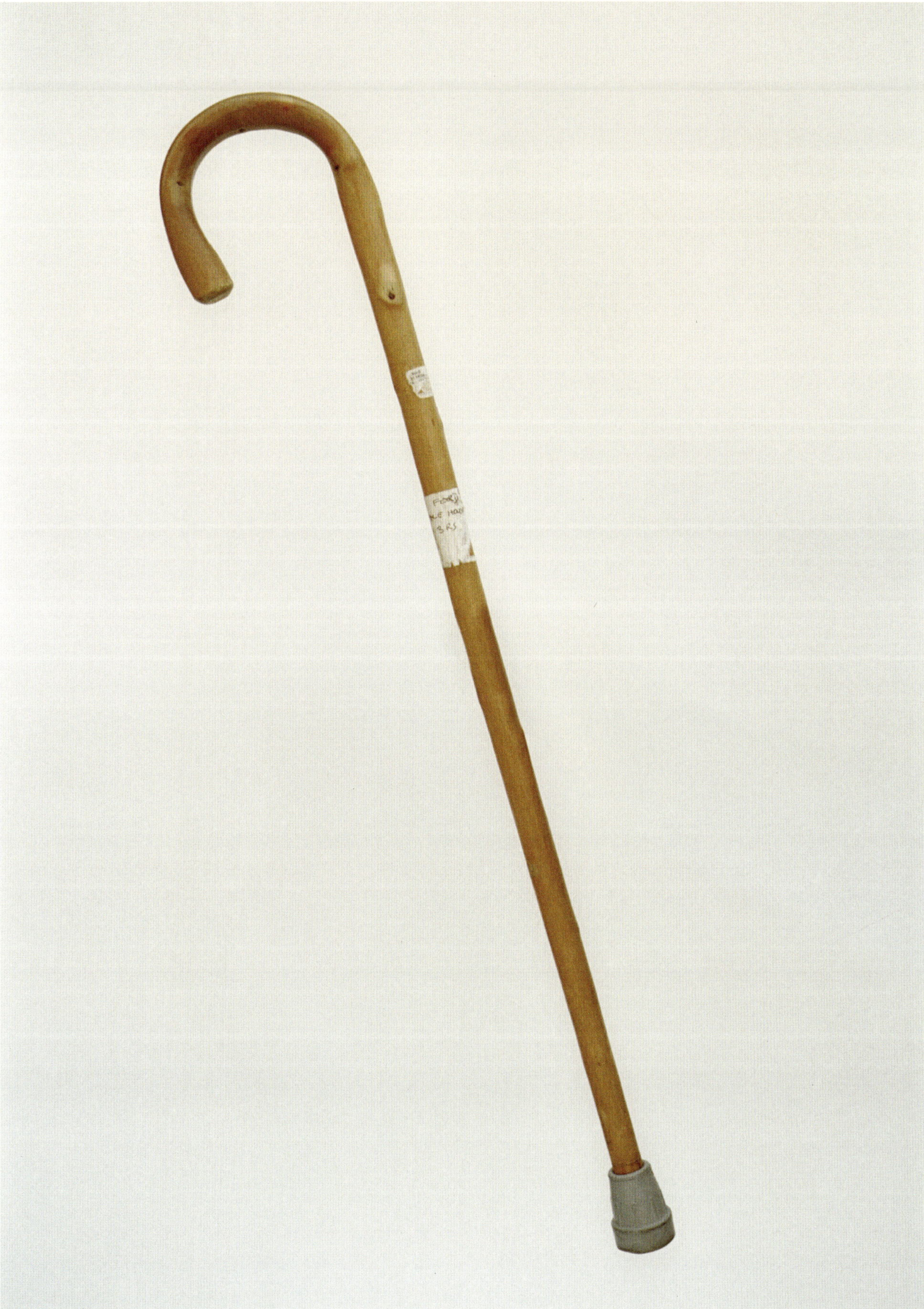

T

Temperance wonders,
'If T is for tea,
Why doesn't honey
Begin with a B?'

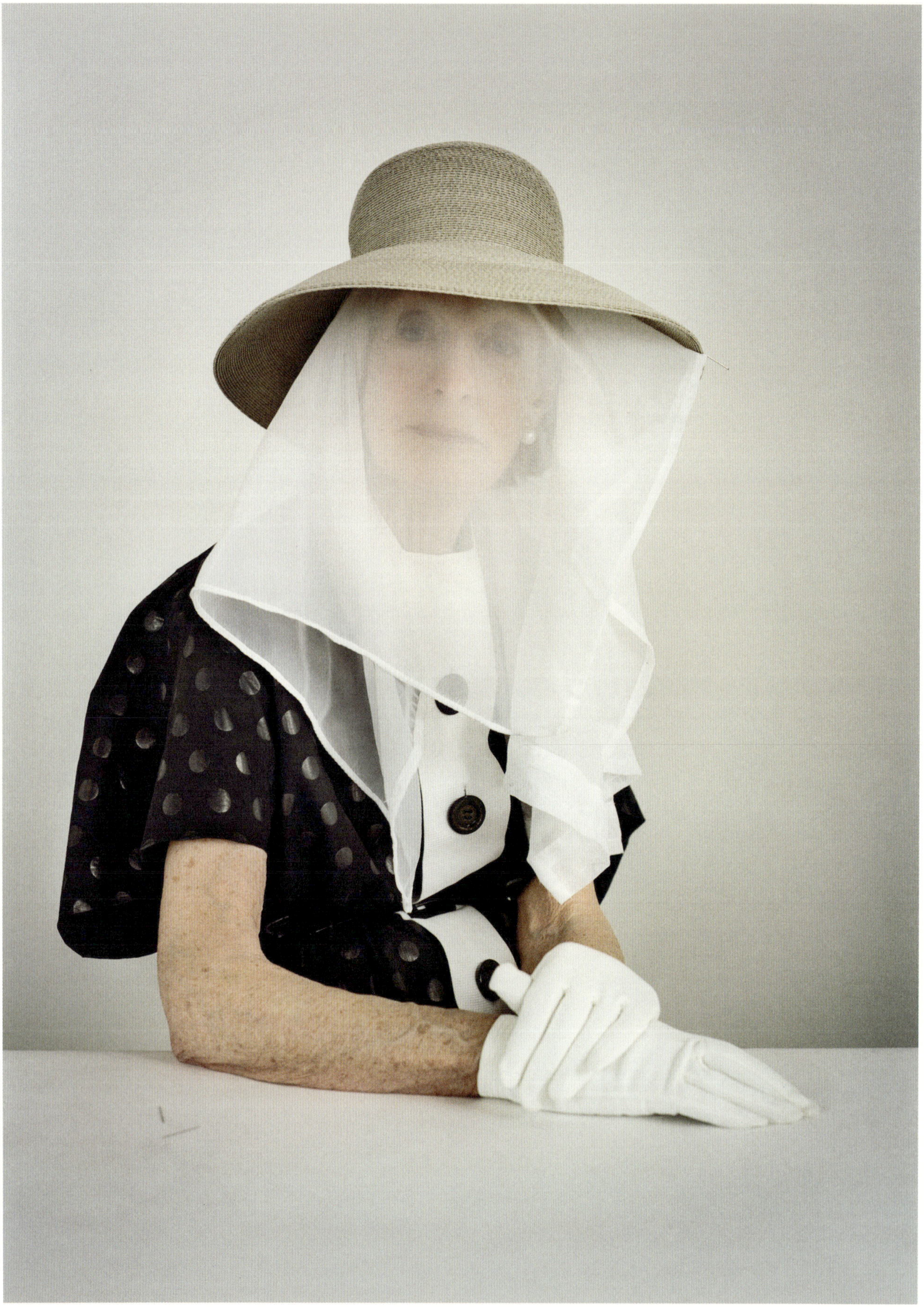

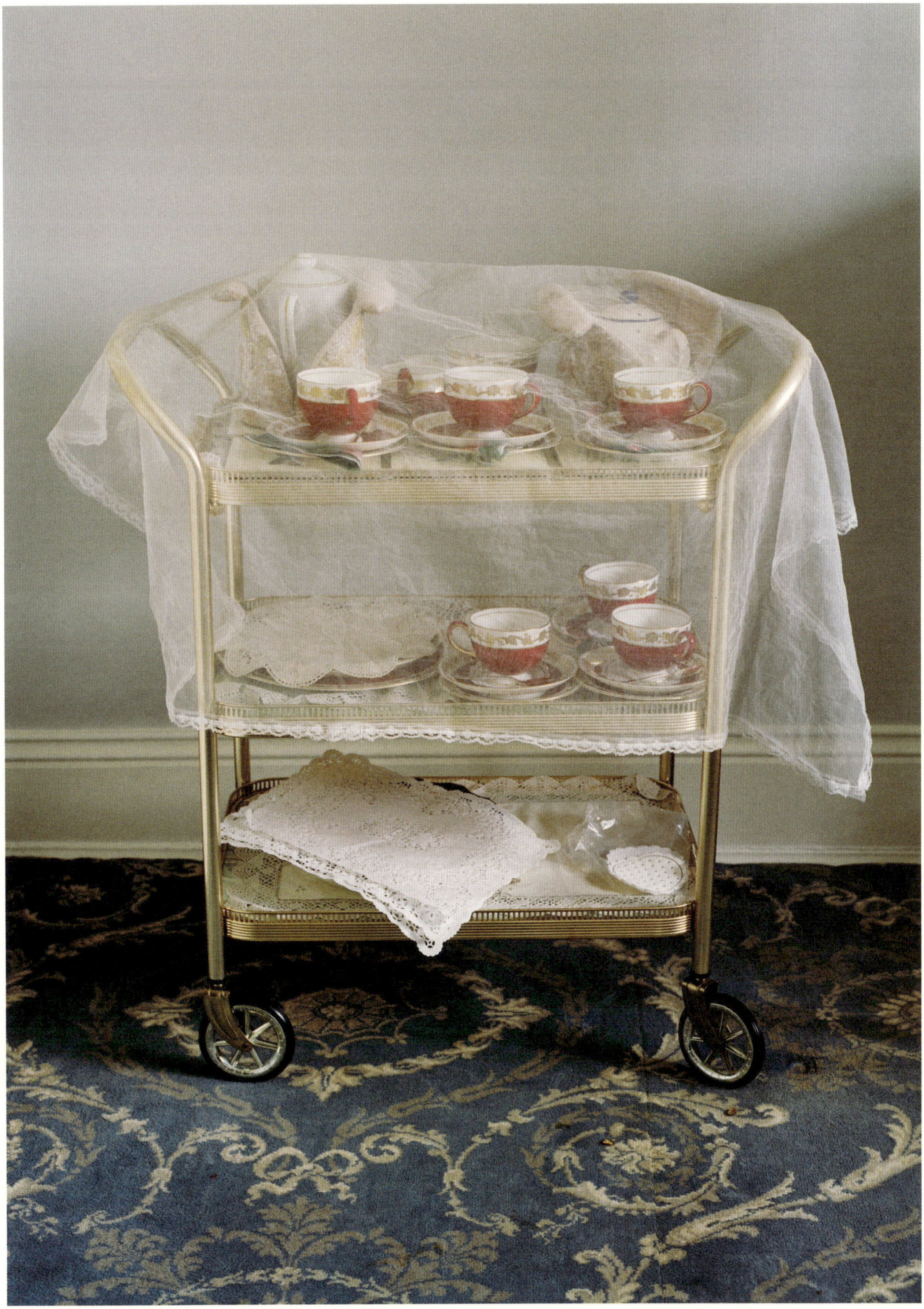

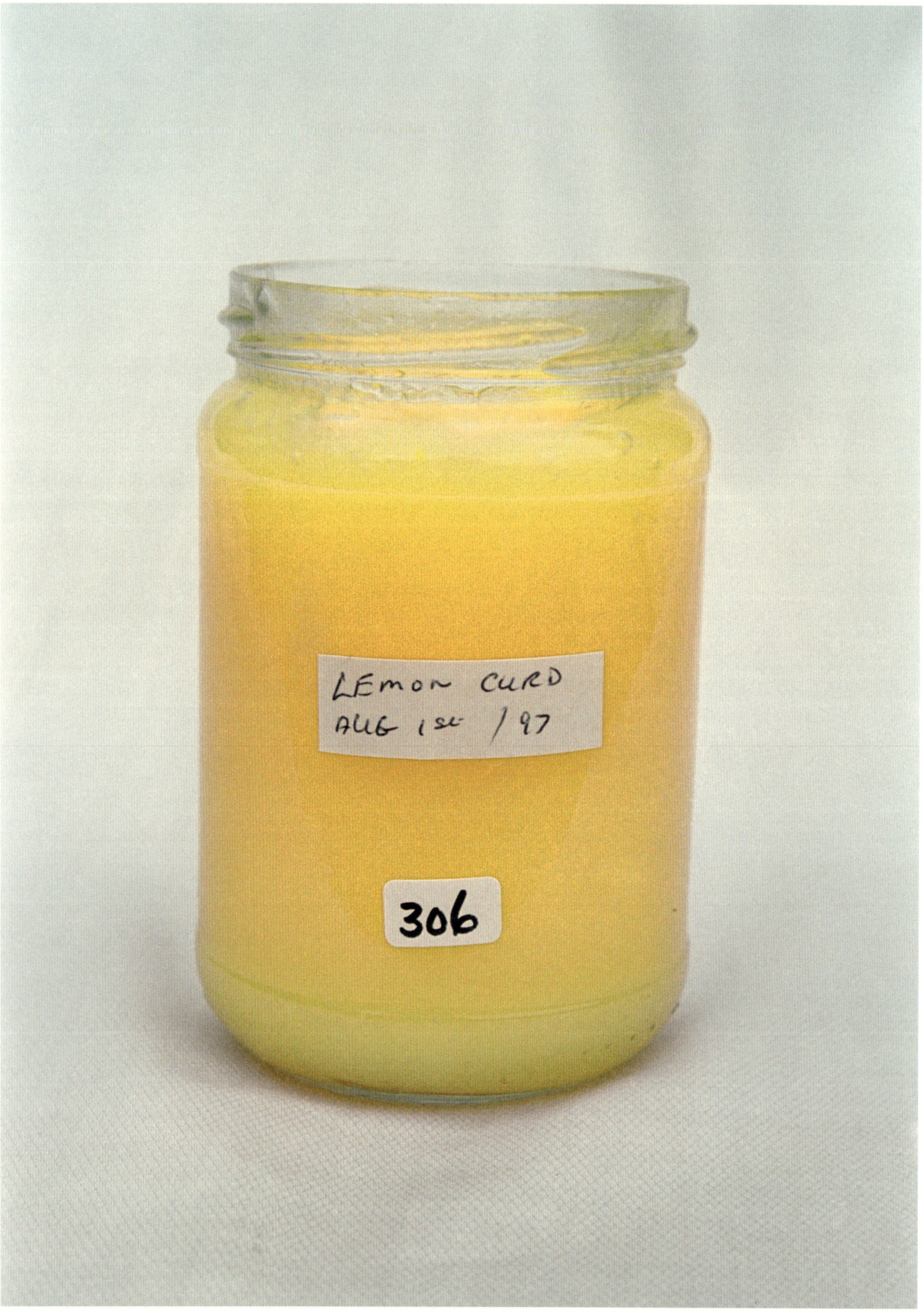
LEMON CURD
AUG 1st / 97
306

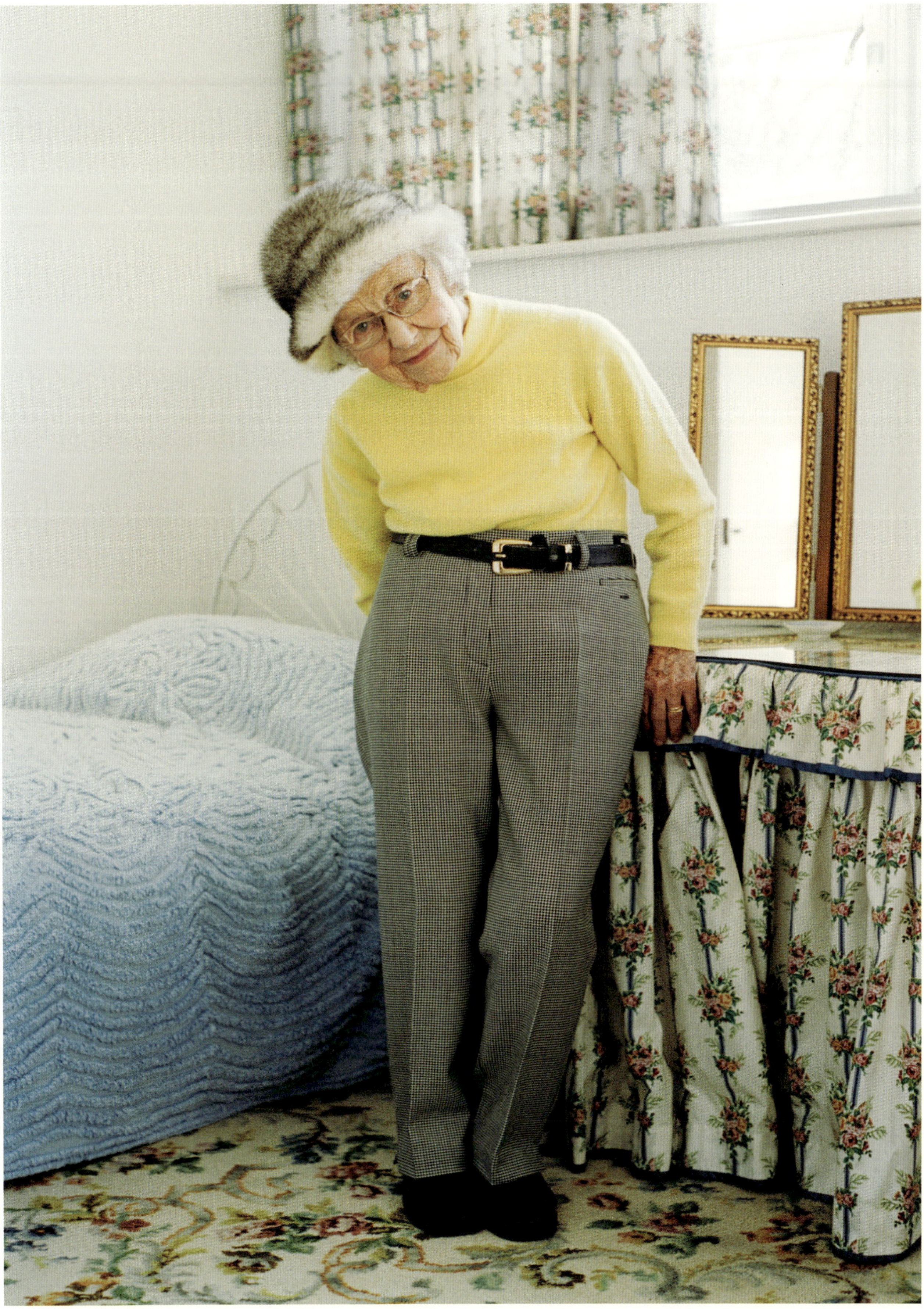

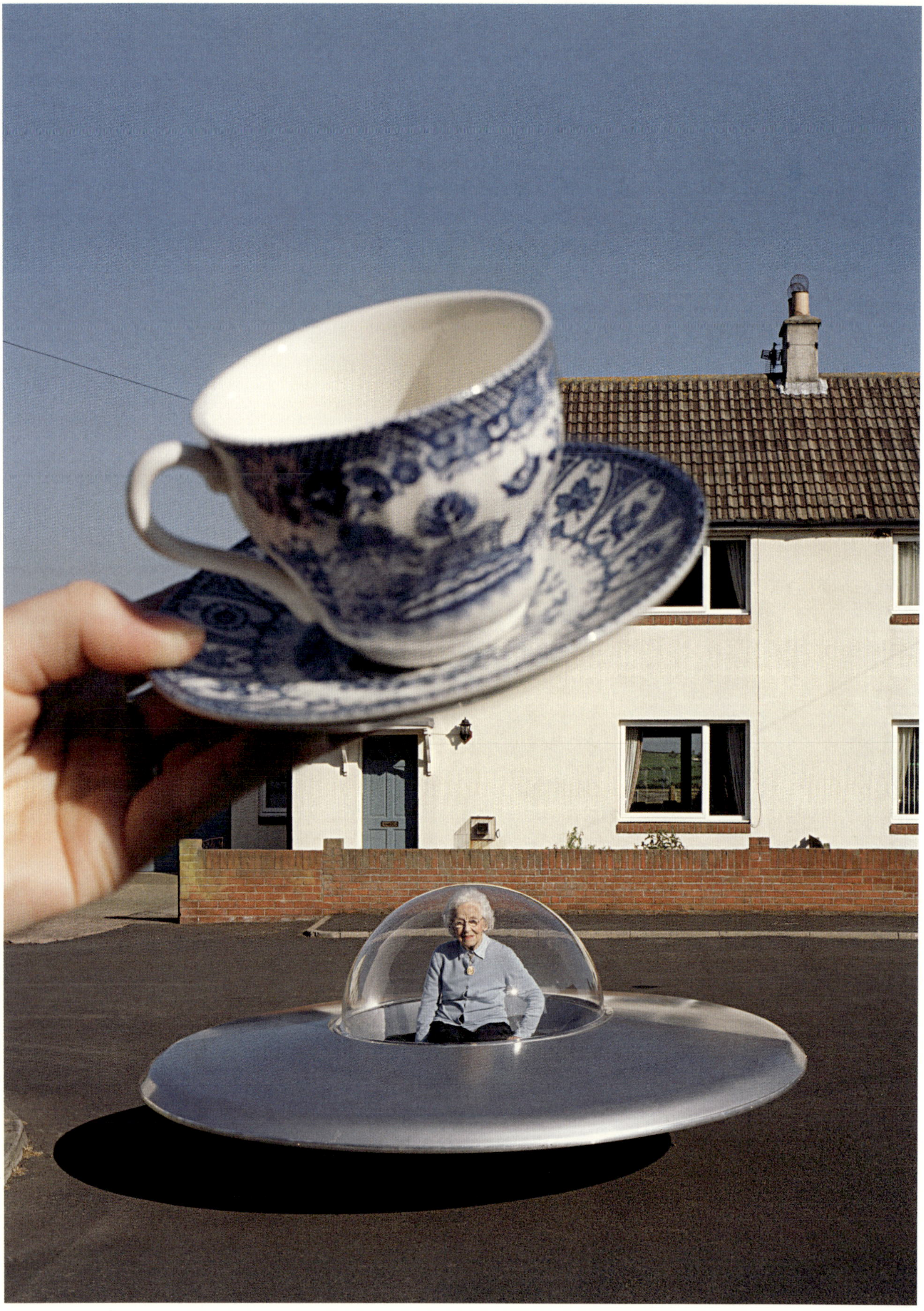

U

Ursula spent Wednesday
On Mars. Did you not know?
She took a flying saucer,
AKA a UFO.

V

Vi's most valiant moment?
The V-sign that she made
To Churchill, at Victoria, in
The VE Day parade.

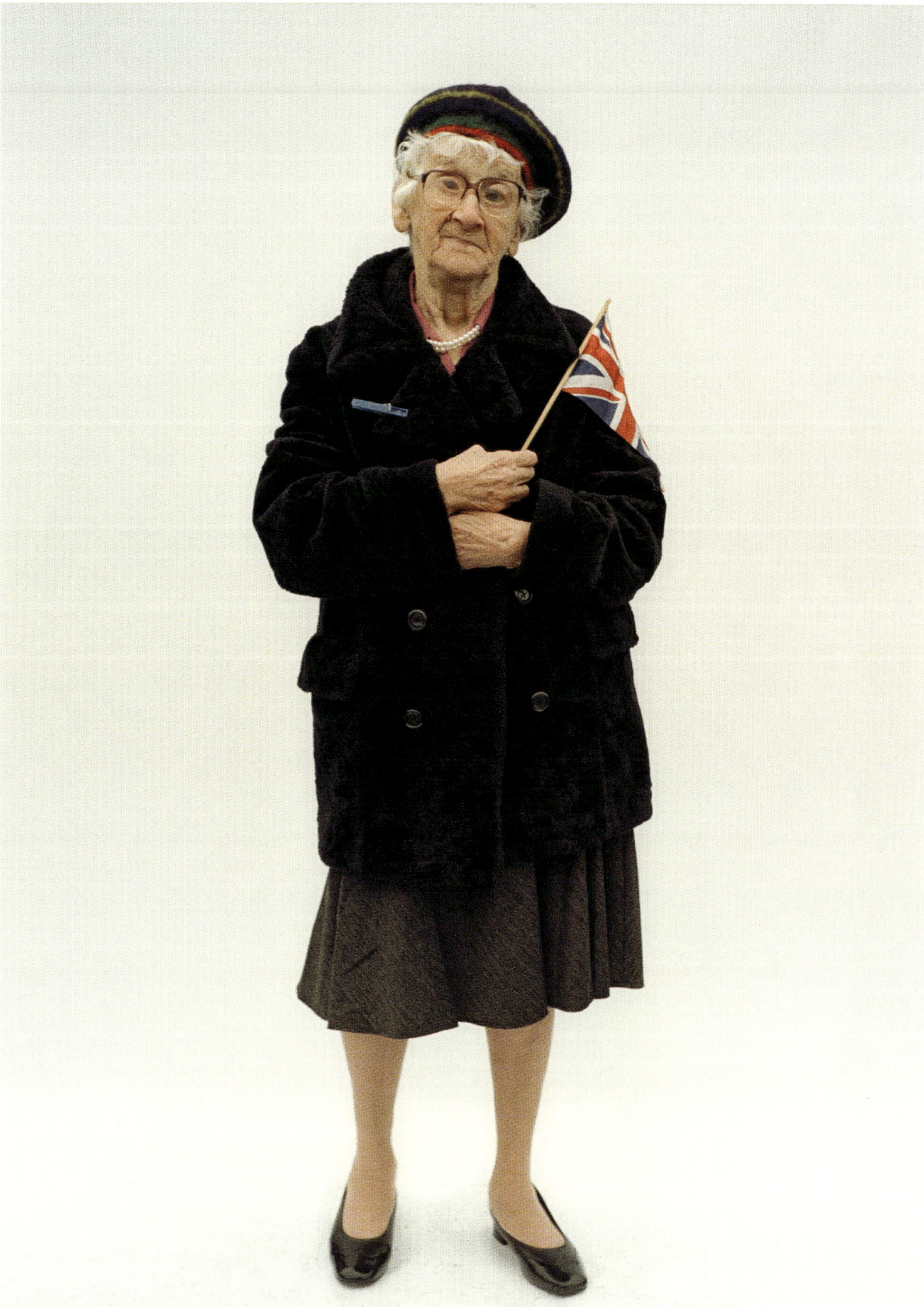

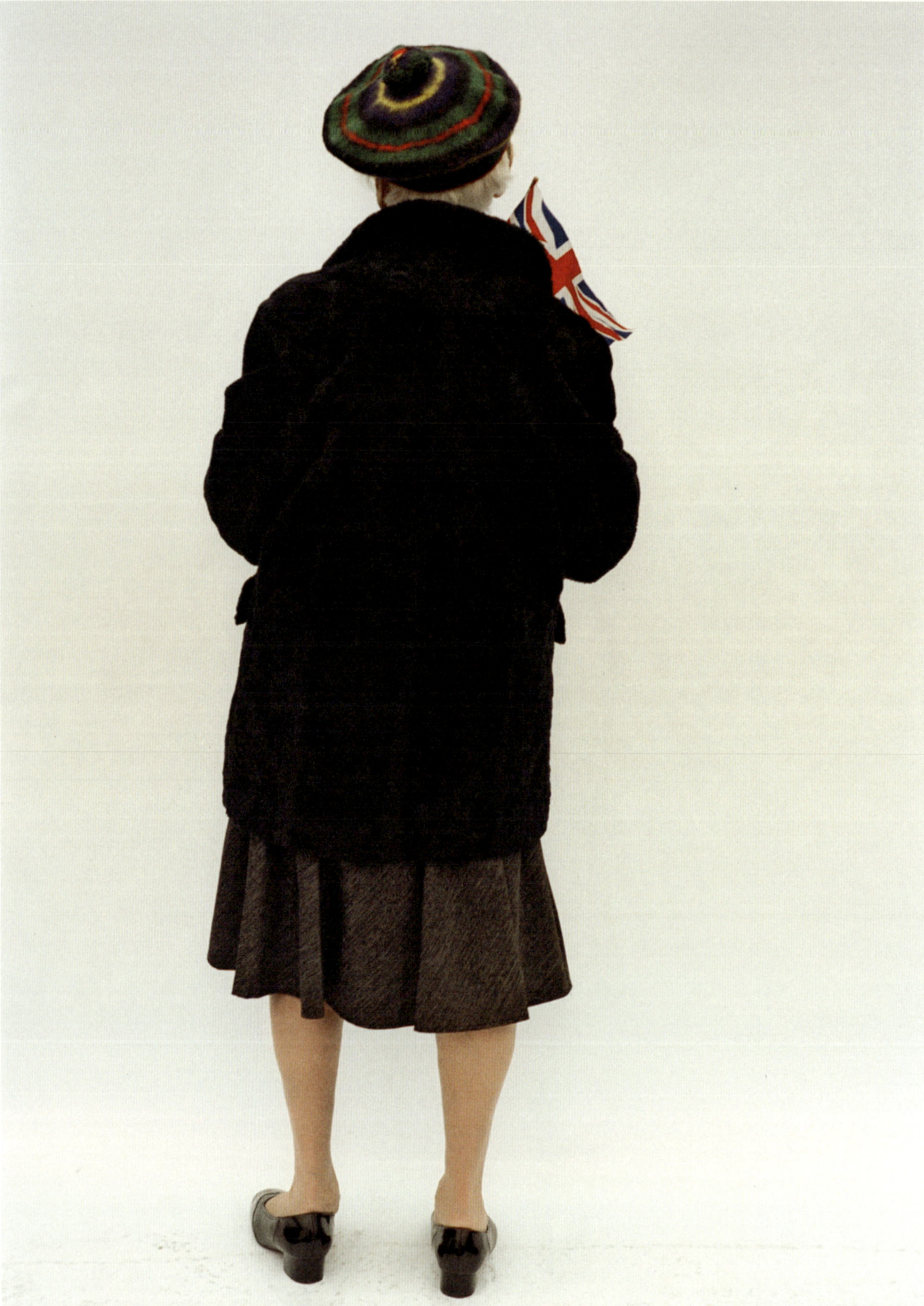

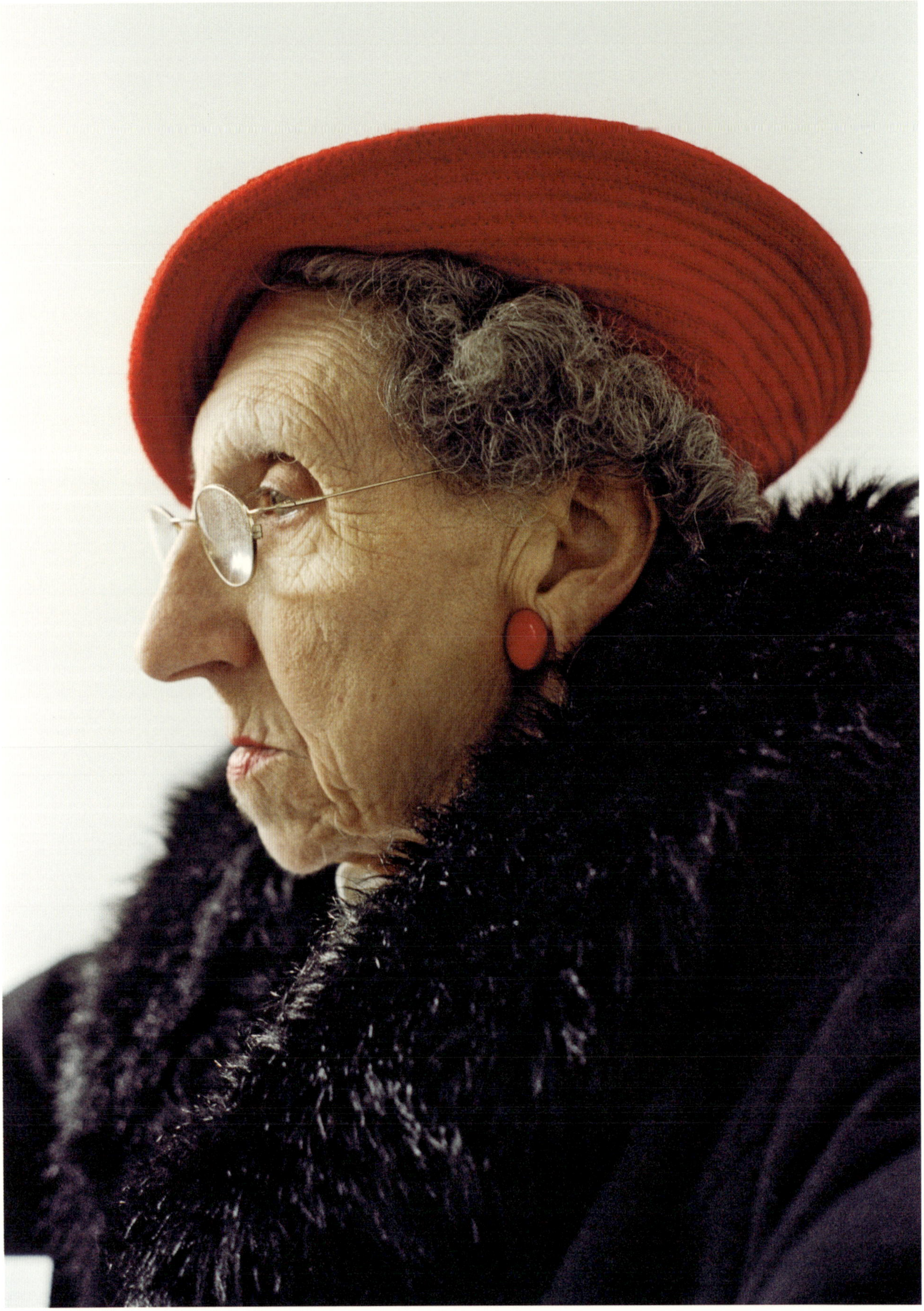

Wilhelmina is a witch,
Although she doesn't look it.
Best not offer her your hand,
She'll chop it off
And cook it.

W

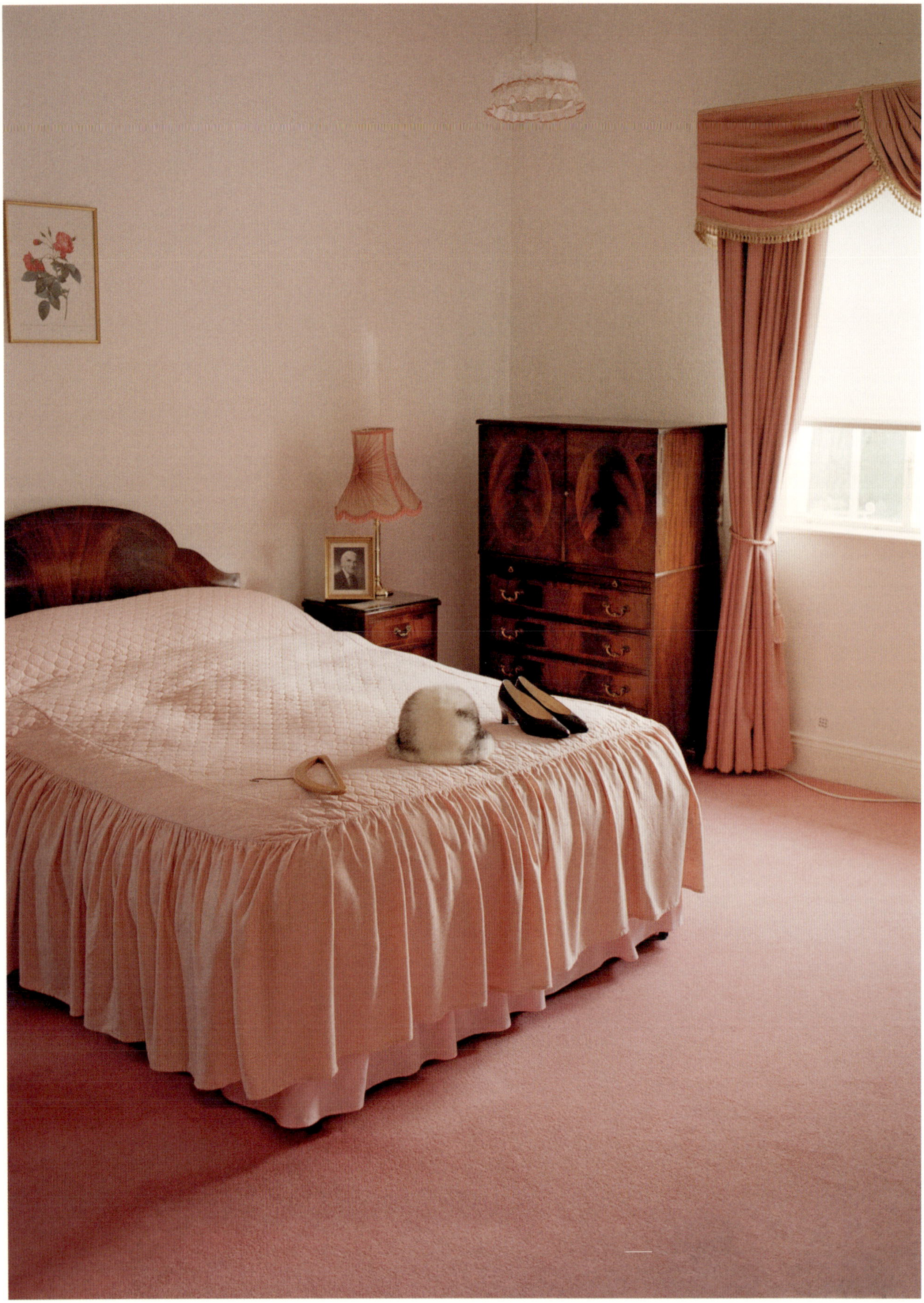

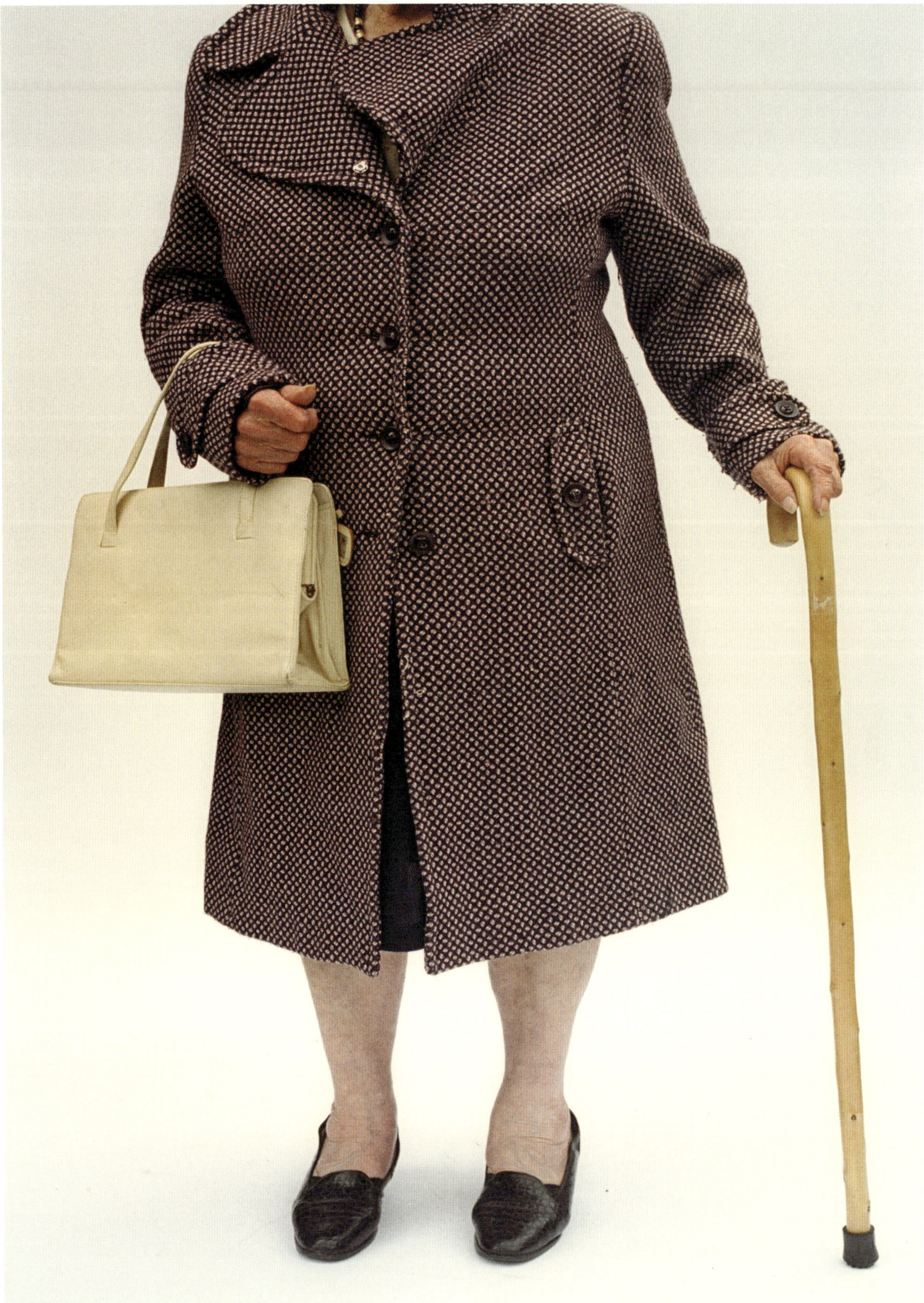

X

X-rays will sort out that hip,
But Xalia's worried sick, as
When they take those photographs,
They might just spot her knickers.

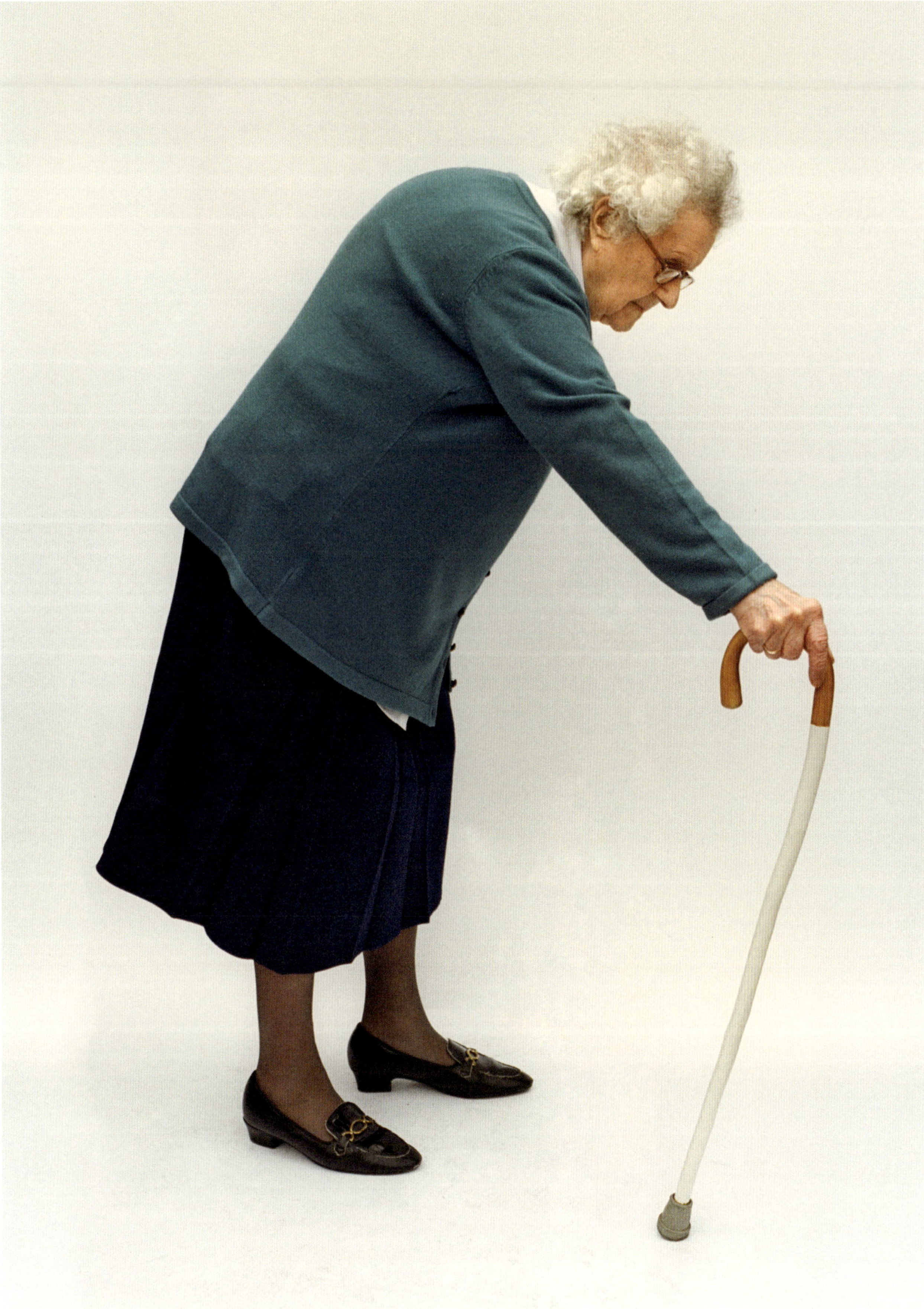

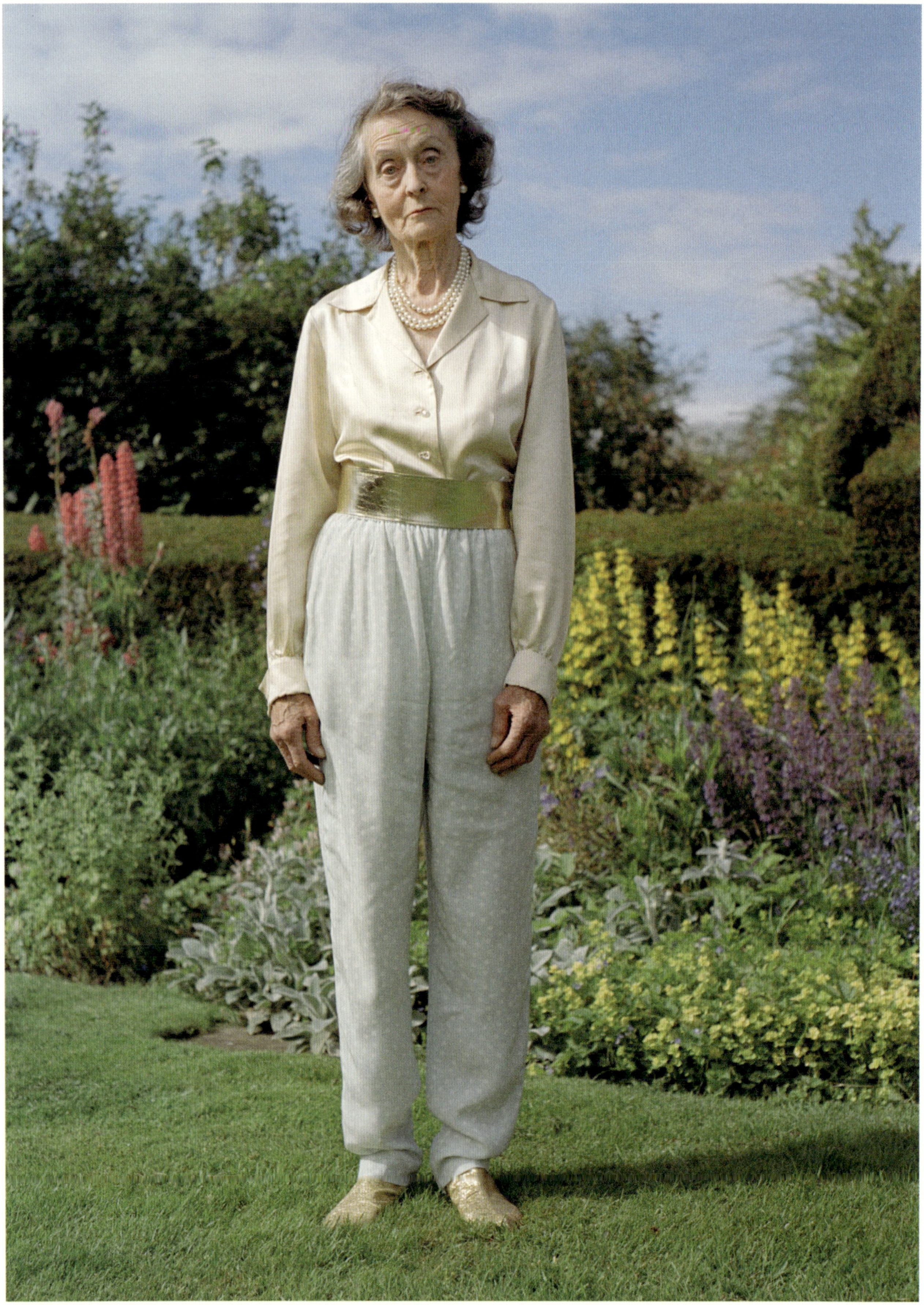

Y

Years fly, thinks Yvonne,
Youth flies too.
Yesterday, thinks Yvonne,
I was you.

Z

Zelda's Zimmerframe's all set
To whisk her off to bed.
Night, night, sleep tight,
Z–Z–Z.

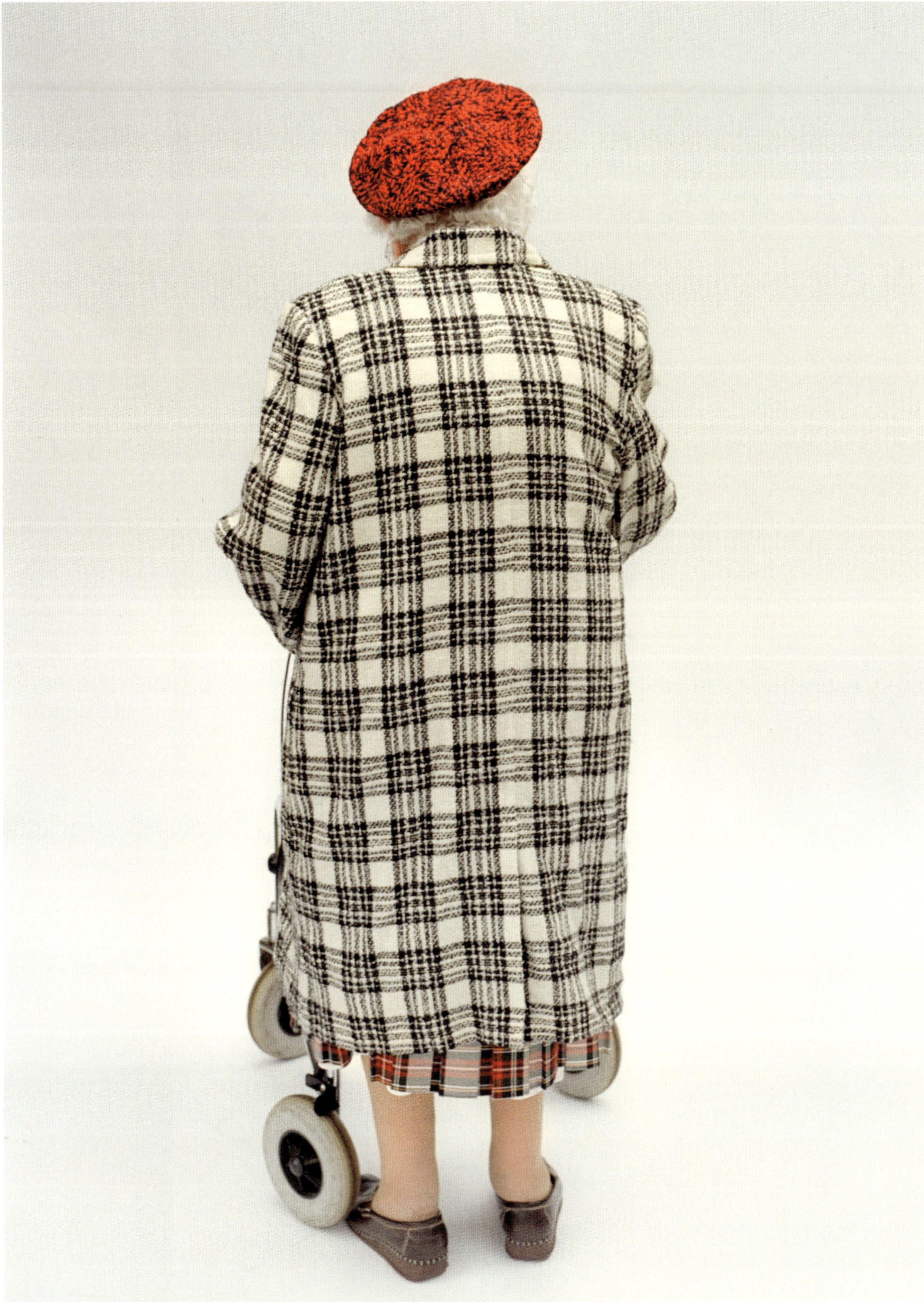

THANK YOU TO...

Lawrence Mynott for his illustrations.
Kit Hesketh-Harvey for his verse.

Ruth Ansel for her book design and art direction.
Bonnie Briant for her assistance in the book's design.
Francesca Foley for casting the grandmothers.
Simon Costin for his set design, as seen on page two.

Rachel Louise Brown and Polly Penrose
at the Tim Walker Studio.
To photographic assistants
Emma Dalzell, Francesca Foley and Alison Tanner.

For film processing, contacting and printing,
thank you to...
Mike Baluk, Eddy Cater,
Graham Cox and Lee Williams
at Rapid Eye.
Cos d'Aprano and Jeremy Ramsden
at Labyrinth.

Graeme Bulcraig, Adam Cook, Ben Pickett,
Kim Stevenson and Emma Williams
at Touch Digital.

Jacob Kjeldgaard
Lorna O'Bryen
Rupert Walker

And thank you, most importantly, to the
individuals who so kindly agreed
to pose for their photographs. Your
generosity has made possible a donation
to the charity Friends of the Elderly.
www.fote.org.uk

ACKNOWLEDGMENTS

First published in the United Kingdom in 2013
by Thames & Hudson Ltd, 181A High Holborn, London WC1V 7QX

The Granny Alphabet
Photographs and Foreword by Tim Walker
Verse by Kit Hesketh-Harvey

Assistant to designer: Bonnie Briant

British Library Cataloguing-in-Publication Data

A catalogue record for this book is available from the British Library

ISBN 978-0-500-54426-6

This is one volume of the two-volume publication *The Granny Alphabet* by Tim Walker

Printed and bound in China by C&C Offset Printing Co. Ltd

To find out about all our publications, please visit www.thamesandhudson.com.
There you can subscribe to our e-newsletter, browse or download our
current catalogue, and buy any titles that are in print.

Design by Ruth Ansel

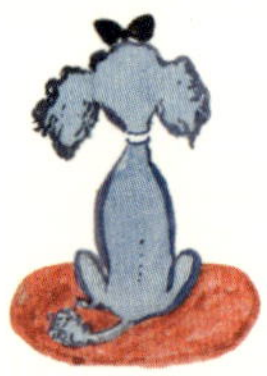

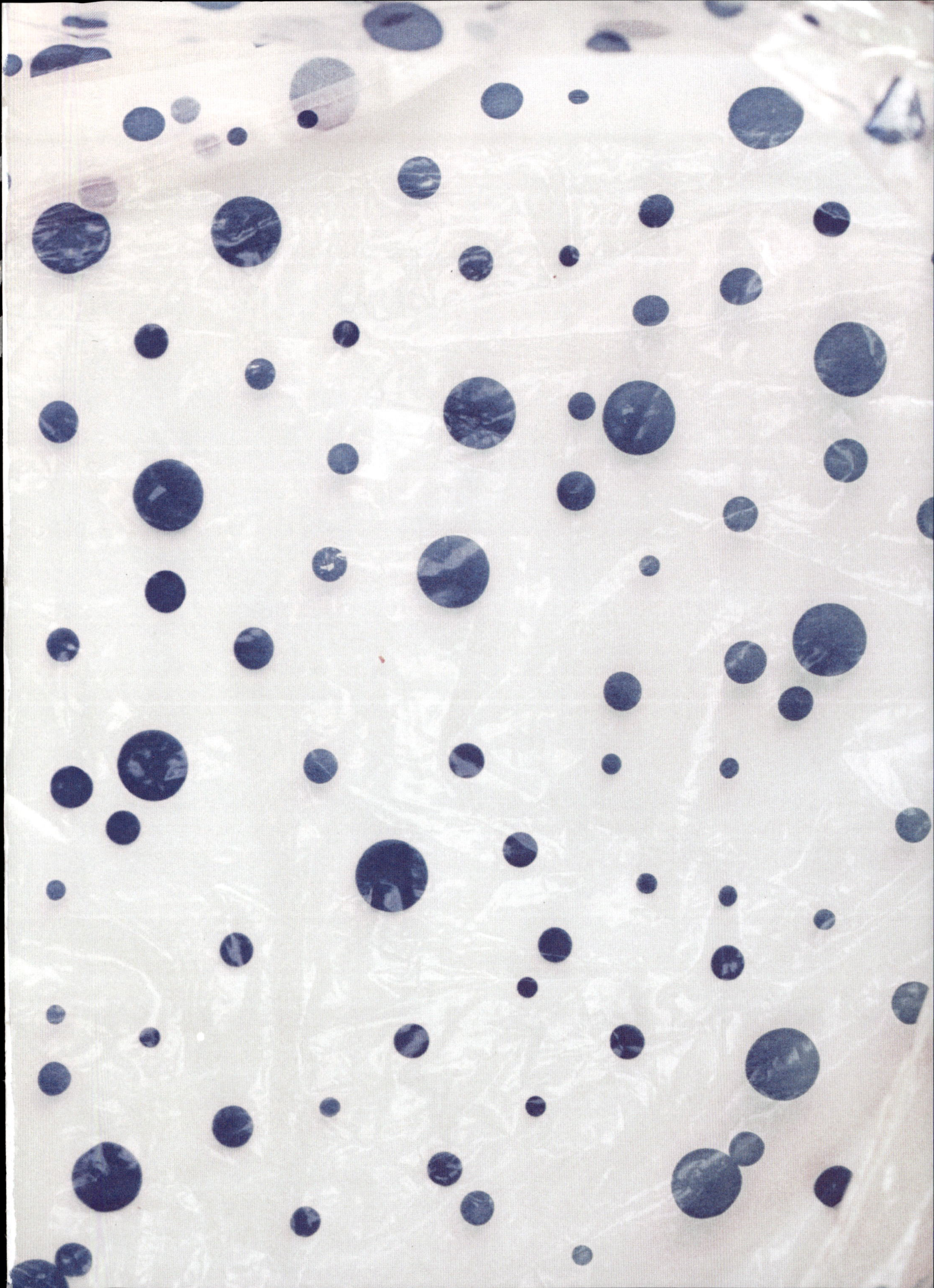

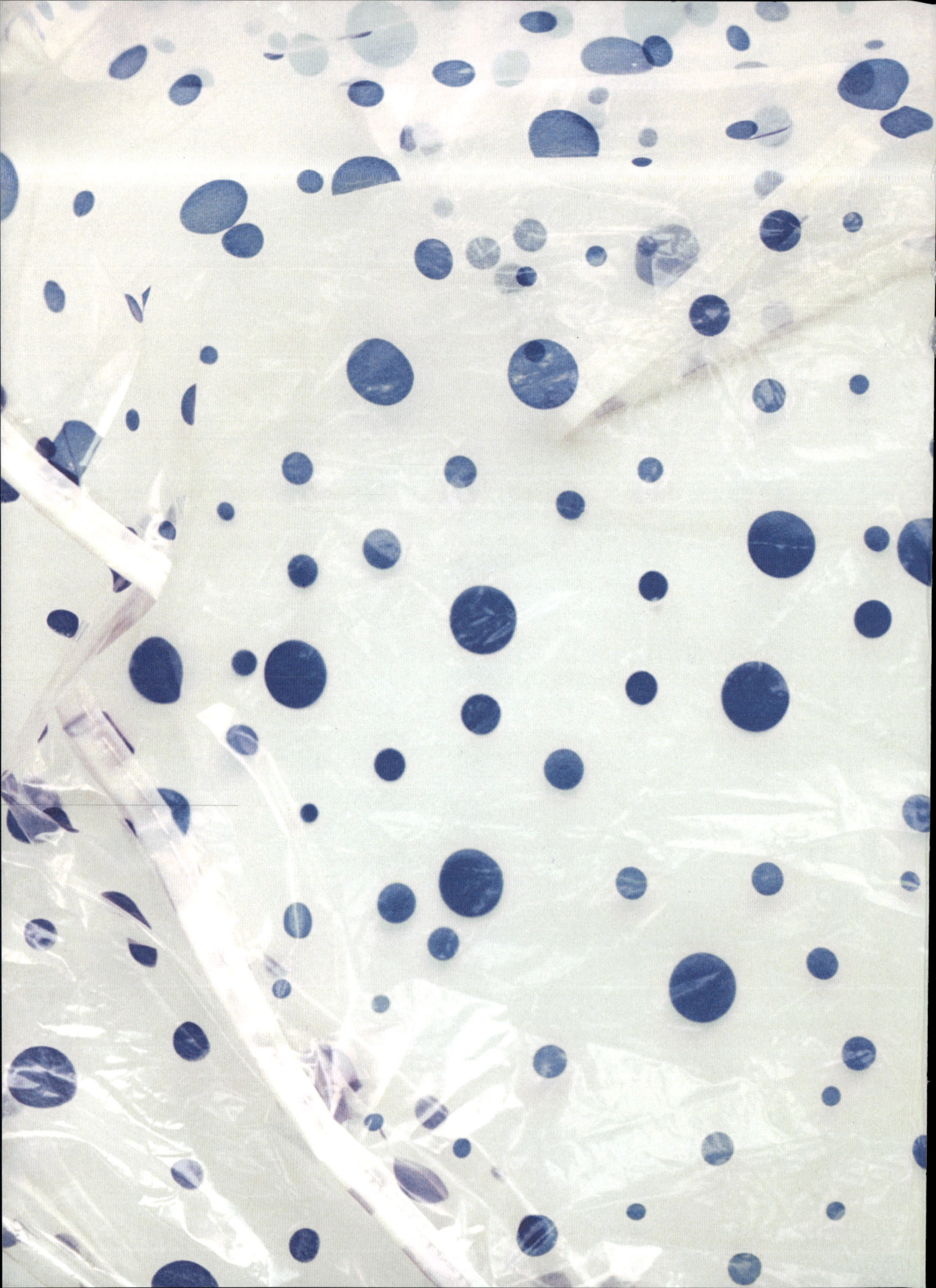